$9.95

11/09/10

B&T

ML

D1111961

CULTURE SMART!
SYRIA

Sarah Standish

PATERSON FREE PUBLIC LIBRARY
250 Broadway
Paterson, New Jersey 07501

·K·U·P·E·R·A·R·D·

This book is available for special discounts for bulk purchases for sales promotions or premiums. Special editions, including personalized covers, excerpts of existing books, and corporate imprints, can be created in large quantities for special needs.

For more information in the USA write to Special Markets/Premium Sales, 1745 Broadway, MD 6–2, New York, NY 10019, or e-mail specialmarkets@randomhouse.com.

In the United Kingdom contact Kuperard publishers at the address below.

ISBN 978 1 85733 526 2
This book is also available as an e-book: eISBN 978 1 85733 563 7

British Library Cataloguing in Publication Data
A CIP catalogue entry for this book is available from the British Library

Copyright © 2010 Kuperard

All rights reserved. No part of this publication may be reprinted or reproduced, stored in a retrieval system, or transmitted in any form or by any means without prior permission in writing from the publishers.

Culture Smart!® is a registered trademark of Bravo Ltd

First published in Great Britain 2010
by Kuperard, an imprint of Bravo Ltd
59 Hutton Grove, London N12 8DS
Tel: +44 (0) 20 8446 2440 Fax: +44 (0) 20 8446 2441
www.culturesmart.co.uk
Inquiries: sales@kuperard.co.uk

Distributed in the United States and Canada
by Random House Distribution Services
1745 Broadway, New York, NY 10019
Tel: +1 (212) 572-2844 Fax: +1 (212) 572-4961
Inquiries: csorders@randomhouse.com

Series Editor Geoffrey Chesler
Design Bobby Birchall

Printed in Malaysia

Cover image: Dome in the Khan Asad Pasha, Damascus. © iStockphoto.com

The photographs on pages 72 and 133 are reproduced by permission of the author.

Photographs on pages 29, 34, 37, 67, 73, 82, 89, 93, 104, 107, 111 and 127 are reproduced by permission of Jillian York: www.flickr.com/photos/jilliancyork/collections/.

Images on these pages reproduced under Creative Commons Attribution Share-Alike licenses 1.0, 2.0, 2.5, and 3.0: 13 © Bertramz; 17 (bottom) © PHGCOM; 19 © Jerzy Strzelecki; 20 From Guillaume Rey, Étude sur les monuments de l'architecture militaire des croisés en Syrie et dans l'île de Chypre (1871); 21 © Godfried Warreyn; 27 © Soman; 92 © Daniel Ersdel; 112 © Bernard Gagnon; 122 © Heretiq; 123 and 125 © Jerzy Strzelecki

Images on the following pages reproduced under Creative Commons Attribution licenses 2.0, 2.5, and 3.0 : 55 © Hendrik Dacquin; 65 and 91 © Bertramz; 106 © Paul Joseph; 121 © seier+seier; and 131 © Shadi Hijazi. Page151 © Ricardo Stuckert/ABr, Creative Commons License Attribution 2.5 Brazil

About the Author

SARAH STANDISH is a writer, translator, and Arabic teacher who currently lives and works in Portland, Oregon. A graduate in Asian and Middle Eastern Studies of Barnard College in New York City, she spent a year living in Syria and studying Arabic literature with the Center for Arabic Study Abroad. She has also spent time in Jordan, Morocco, Egypt, and Lebanon. In Portland, she works for a nonprofit aid agency, teaches Arabic at local colleges, and does freelance translation. In her spare time, she enjoys reading, biking, traveling, and watching Syrian television shows.

The Culture Smart! series is continuing to expand.
For further information and latest titles visit
www.culturesmartguides.com

The publishers would like to thank **CultureSmart!**Consulting for its help in researching and developing the concept for this series.

CultureSmart!Consulting creates tailor-made seminars and consultancy programs to meet a wide range of corporate, public-sector, and individual needs. Whether delivering courses on multicultural team building in the USA, preparing Chinese engineers for a posting in Europe, training call-center staff in India, or raising the awareness of police forces to the needs of diverse ethnic communities, it provides essential, practical, and powerful skills worldwide to an increasingly international workforce.

For details, visit www.culturesmartconsulting.com

CultureSmart!Consulting and **CultureSmart!** guides have both contributed to and featured regularly in the weekly travel program "Fast Track" on BBC World TV.

contents

contents

Map of Syria

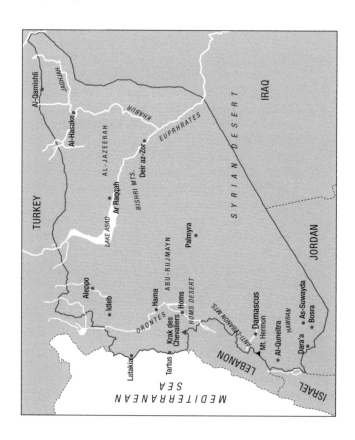

introduction

To get to know Syria is to become acquainted with one of the most rewarding destinations in the Middle East. Its historic attractions are stunning, and the Syrians are gracious and welcoming hosts; you can expect to be treated like a person, and not just a tourist. This book is based on the idea that you can gain as much from a little insight into contemporary Syrian culture as you can from its rich and fascinating past. Even if you don't spend a lot of time in the country, it should help you to understand what you see, and to interact more meaningfully and easily with the Syrians you meet.

Of course, there are always thorns with the roses: Syria's economy is inefficient, and its youth frustrated; the strong-man political system has held the country together in times of severe strife, but discouraged the development of a vibrant, public intellectual life. Syrians value education, but they're more likely to spend their free time watching television than reading. Their strong sense of tradition has preserved some of the bad along with the good, so society remains highly patriarchal and women face a strict double standard.

Despite such drawbacks, this is a country that's wealthy not only in resources, but also, and especially, in its people. Syrians remember that friends and family are just as important as ambition, and they show it. They're also welcoming to strangers, and eager to display their famous hospitality. Call for help on the street in Syria, and you'll get it; ask for directions, and you'll as likely as not find someone ready to walk with you to your destination. Chat with a stranger, and you may find yourself being invited home for coffee. Syrians are patient, meeting life's challenges with a sense of readiness and even optimism. When there's an occasion that can be celebrated with singing and dancing, they will seize the opportunity. They also have a deep pride in their country, both in its rich heritage and in the fact that international brands are now in the stores. Political activism may be stifled, but young Syrians debate with passion in private over what they want their country to become—and how they can help to bring it there. Last but not least, Syrians will never stop surprising you: get to know a few, and they may turn the stereotypes inside out several times over.

This book looks at Syria's long history and its present-day political realities. It describes the many subgroups that make up the population, with their individual customs, as well as what unites the Syrians—their strong family lives, the value they place on friends, and the ways they spend their free time. There are tips for traveling and on what to expect when conducting business. You'll learn how Syrians communicate with each other, and how you can communicate with them, along with a few Arabic phrases to help you get around.

Culture Smart! Syria aims to help you make the most of your visit, though of course the best things about the country can't be contained in one small volume. They're what you'll experience there!

Key Facts

Official Name	Syrian Arab Republic	Al-Jumhuriyyah al-Arabiyyah as-Suriyyah
Capital City	Damascus	
Major Cities	Aleppo, Latakia	
Population	22 million (2010 est.)	20,000 Syrians also live in the occupied Golan Heights.
Ethnic Makeup	Arab 90.3%, Kurds, Armenians, and other 9.7%	
Age Structure	0–14 years: 35.8%; 15–64 years: 60.4%; 65 years and over: 3.8%	
Area	71,498 sq. miles (185,180 sq. km)	500 sq. miles (1,295 sq. km) occupied by Israel
Geography	Located in Western Asia; bordered by Lebanon, Turkey, Iraq, Jordan, Israeli-occupied Golan Heights, and the Mediterranean Sea.	
Terrain	Semi-arid plateau with mountains; coastal plain along Mediterranean	
Climate	Hot, dry summers and mild, rainy winters. Inland desert is dryer; coastal climate is milder.	
Natural Resources	Petroleum, phosphates, chrome and manganese ores, asphalt, iron ore, rock salt, marble, gypsum, hydropower	

Currency	Syrian Pounds (SP). Called "Lira" in Arabic	
Language	Official language is Arabic; Kurdish, Armenian, and other languages spoken among minority ethnic groups; Aramaic spoken in a few villages.	English and other European languages spoken by those who work or live in areas that bring them into contact with foreigners; more common among youth and in urban areas
Religion	Sunni Muslim 74%; Muslims minorities (including Alawites and Druze) 16%; Christian 10%	A small number of Jews live in Damascus and Aleppo.
Government	Formally, a unicameral republic where the President is head of state and is approved by referendum every seven years.	In practice, a dictatorship dominated by one party and the military.
Media	There are several local newspapers and television channels, both privately owned and government-run.	Satellite television is the most popular form of media.
Electricity	220 volts, 50 Hz	European 2-pronged plugs used
Internet	.sy	
Telephone	Syria's country code is 963.	Dial 00 to call out of Syria.
Time Zone	GMT +2 hrs GMT +3 hrs in the summer	

LAND &
PEOPLE

Syria has the dubious distinction of nestling between some of the biggest names in the news headlines: Iraq to the east, Lebanon and the Mediterranean to the west, Turkey to the north, and Jordan and the Israeli-occupied Golan Heights to the south. But rather than let the turmoil of some of these hot spots spill over its borders, Syria's leaders have tried to make lemonade out of the lemons of a tricky geographical location, positioning the country as a major player in any possible attempt to reshape the Middle East. Henry Kissinger once said of the situation with Israel: "There will be no war without Egypt and no peace without Syria." Syria seems to agree, and will use its position in the region to its best advantage. Syria, however, is also patient: with more than five thousand years of history and a leader who serves for life, it can afford to wait for the best time to act.

GEOGRAPHY

Syria's geographical location has long made it a place of regional and even worldwide significance: its historical status as a nexus between Mediterranean ports and Asian trade routes made it a meeting place of merchants, goods, and cultures, and its capital city, Damascus, is the oldest continually inhabited urban center in the world. Historically, the area known as "Syria" once encompassed modern-day Lebanon, Palestine, Jordan, and southern Turkey, but grand schemes and strokes of colonial pens after the First World War shaved the country down to its current 71,498 square miles (185,180 sq. km). Today, its twenty million inhabitants are mostly distributed in a wide crescent that arcs from the southern right-hand border with Jordan, then reaches up to the western border with Lebanon, before curving eastward along the northern border with Turkey. This crescent enjoys the most temperate climate and the best arable lands, while the remaining triangle to the east is an unwelcoming desert whose temperatures are much more extreme.

Contrary to the stereotypical picture of Middle Eastern geography, only about one-fifth of Syria is actually classified as desert. Another portion is semiarid, and other regions can be positively verdant—particularly the plain along the Mediterranean coast, which includes the regionally

important port city of Latakia. The lush vegetation that covers this plain continues into the Jabal an-Nusayriyah mountain range that parallels the coast. A pass called the Homs Gap separates this range from the Anti-Lebanon mountains along the Syria-Lebanon border to the south; as the easiest way from the interior to the coast, the pass was historically a focal point of both trade routes and invasions. Just east of the Jabal an-Nusayriyah, the Orontes River flows north through the al-Ghab plain, separating the first mountain range from another, Jabal az-Zawiya. The moderately sized cities of Hama and Homs both lie near the Orontes.

The southernmost region of Syria, including the Israeli-occupied Golan Heights, is known as the Hawran. It's a plateau, edged in the east by the dormant volcanoes that form the Jabal al-Arab range (also known as Jabal ad-Druz), and its regionally important cities include as-Suwayda and Dara'a. This fertile region, fed by rainfall and the springs that give rise to the Yarmuk River, is sometimes called "the breadbasket of Syria."

Inland and to the north of these mountain ranges is a semiarid steppe, intersected by a small mountain chain. Here, the Barada River that flows from the Anti-Lebanon mountains gave rise to the al-Ghuta Oasis upon which Damascus is built. This oasis once surrounded the city with a ring of greenery, but in the past few decades this has mostly been obliterated by urban sprawl.

To the east lies the expansive desert region, relatively unpopulated but bordered in the north by the Euphrates, the largest and most important river in Syria, which provides some 80 percent of the country's water resources. In 1973, the Syrian government completed the ath-Thawra dam on the river, creating a large reservoir known as Lake Asad. The dam and reservoir provide electricity and water reserves for the country, but use and misuse of the Euphrates's waters has been a continuing point of contention with Turkey—where the river originates, fed by springs and snowmelt—and Iraq—into which it subsequently flows. The triangle to the northeast of the Euphrates is known as the Jazeerah, or Island, and is an area of great agricultural significance. The Jazeerah's regionally important cities include Deir az-Zor, Hasake, and Qamishli. To the west of Lake Asad lies the city of Aleppo, an ancient trading center almost as old as Damascus—some say even older.

Its diverse geography means that Syria is home to an equally diverse people: something that can lead to division, but is also a source of cultural wealth.

CLIMATE

Weather patterns vary across the country, ranging from the hot, dry summers inland to warm, humid summers on the coast; winters can be chilly and dry on the coast, and more biting inland, with ferocious though infrequent rains. Luckily for Syrians and their guests, summers can even be cool in the mountains, making these popular escapes for day trips. In Damascus, temperatures range from an average of 64–99°F (18–37°C) in August to an average of 36–57°F (2–12°C) in January. The coast tends to enjoy milder weather, while the desert climate is more extreme, in addition to being struck by sandstorms in the spring. Syria has suffered from a severe drought over the past several years that endangers the livelihoods of its farmers.

PEOPLE

Historically Syria's population has been mainly rural, but the past few decades have witnessed a degree of urbanization that now places more than half the country's people in cities. The population is also young, with more than one-third under fourteen years old, and fairly well educated, as four-fifths of the country is literate—a number that's higher for the younger generation.

Its mountainous topography has made Syria the adopted home of a number of minorities who, in the past, took refuge in higher elevations—most notably, the Alawites in the coastal mountains and the Druze in the Jabal al-Arab to the south. While primarily Sunni Muslim, Syria is also home to numerous other religious minorities, including Shi'a Muslim Isma'ilis, Yazidis, some thirteen Christian sects, and the elderly remnants of a once-vibrant Jewish community. Most Syrians are Arab, but ethnic minorities include Kurds, Armenians, Assyrians, and Syrian Turkmen.

A word of caution about categorizing Syrians primarily by religion or ethnicity: identity in Syria is multifaceted and may incorporate allegiance not only to sect or ethnic group but also to town or city of birth, region within Syria, Syria as a nation-state, pan-Arabism, social class, gender, political ideology, and more. Nonetheless, religious identity and the specter of sectarianism remains such a touchy subject for the government that precise statistics on the country's faith composition are nonexistent; most are merely informed estimates. Roughly speaking, about 74 percent of the population are Sunni Muslims; 16 percent are Muslim minority sects; and 10 percent are Christian. Ethnically, 90 percent are Arab, and most of the remaining 10 percent are Kurds.

A BRIEF HISTORY
Ancient Civilizations

Syria has been home to a succession of ancient civilizations reaching back thousands of years: agriculture was practiced there as early as 12,000 years ago by the Mesolithic Natufian culture, and

archaeological discoveries indicate that the port city of Ugarit (today Ras ash-Shamra, near Latakia) was flourishing in 6000 BCE. In the east, the city of Mari was inhabited from 5000 BCE by the Sumerians and Amorites, and dating to around 3000 BCE was the city-state Ebla to the west, part of an ancient Semitic empire that was subsequently overrun by the Akkadians. During the first two millennia BCE, parts of Syria were conquered by the Canaanites, Phoenicians, Aramaeans, Ancient Egyptians, Mitannians, Assyrians, Babylonians, Hittites, and Persians.

In 333 BCE Alexander the Great conquered Syria, which then became subject to dynastic rule by the descendants of Alexander's general Seleucus. In 64 BCE, Rome annexed Syria as a province which prospered under her rule, connecting the rest of the empire to key eastern trade routes; several Roman emperors, such as Elagabalus and Philip the Arab, could boast of Syrian origins. This period also gave rise to an enduring historical icon: Queen Zenobia, the wife of the ruler of the Roman protectorate of Palmyra (in present-day Syria's eastern desert), who assumed leadership of the state in 267 CE after her husband's murder. Zenobia's army conquered Syria before she invaded Egypt and proclaimed her son emperor— although his young age at the time meant that she herself stood to gain the most. Rome quickly struck back, recapturing the territory and carting off Zenobia in chains to Rome; multiple competing theories about the nature of her death have not prevented her being immortalized as a symbol of beauty, independence, and strength. Syria continued to be an outlying province of the empire after its capital moved to Constantinople. The waning strength of the Byzantine Empire (as it became known) made it possible for foreign incursions—particularly by the Persians—to nibble at Syria's edges, and the area changed hands decisively in the Arab invasion of 640.

Islamic Era and Caliphates: 640–1516

Islam was born in the Arabian Peninsula, at Mecca in present-day Saudi Arabia, and quickly overcame resistance by the local polytheistic tribes before expanding across the rest of the Peninsula and then moving beyond. Syria was the young Arab army's first conquest outside its native environment. The Arabs easily routed the Byzantine army, then relocated their capital from Mecca to Damascus, where the Christian population welcomed them as a relief from the heavy hand of Constantinople's intervention in religious disputes. The Umayyad state established there in 661 was the second Muslim caliphate in history and the first to be established on a dynastic principle. With Syria as its most central and wealthiest province, the caliphate oversaw such an enormous territorial expansion that, by its end in 750 CE, it reached across North Africa and into the Iberian Peninsula to the west, while touching the edges of India in the east. The Umayyad caliphs built an effective professional army, a navy, and a government bureaucracy, including a working postal service, and several buildings of lasting architectural significance, but they did not interfere in the day-to-day governance of Syria, instead delegating authority to their provincial governors; nor did they attempt to convert Syrians to Islam. The Islamic law under which they ruled applied only to Muslim subjects, while adherents of other Abrahamic faiths—Christians and Jews—paid a special tax in exchange for the freedom to continue following their own customary law and traditions.

Syria was relegated to the status of an outlying province under the subsequent Abbasid caliphate, which overthrew the Umayyads in 750 and recentered itself in Baghdad; Syria suffered a consequent period of decline and neglect, punctuated by the occasional invasion and rebellion. Some local Syrian principalities asserted their independence from the Abbasids, beginning with the Aleppo-based Hamdani dynasty that gained control over northern Syria in the ninth century and excelled in scientific achievement. From the west, the Isma'ili Fatimid caliphate moved out of Egypt to conquer Damascus in 970 and exercised a tenuous domination interspersed with Byzantine forays that reconquered parts of Syria in the tenth century, before being forced back by the invading Seljuk Turks in the middle of the twelfth century.

The First Crusade in 1097 also touched Syria, with the Crusaders establishing principalities at Tripoli (in modern-day Lebanon and historical

Syria), Antioch, and Edessa (in today's southern Turkey). While some local leaders initially formed alliances with them, elite and popular resentment against the Crusaders gradually grew and such opportunism was rejected. The Second Crusade suffered a serious defeat when it attempted to take Damascus in 1148. Nur ad-Din, a Seljuk prince in Aleppo, came to Damascus's aid during the siege and then annexed the city in 1154. Under his rule, the city began to enjoy a revival. Not long afterward, in 1187, Saladin recaptured Jerusalem, drove the Europeans from most of their holdings, and then unified Syria and Egypt under the dynasty

that he founded,
the Ayyubids.
The Crusaders,
however, were
not completely
banished from
Syria until
the Mamluk
Sultan Baybars'
military campaign
of 1261–77. This
eradicated all but

a memory of what had occasionally been a
relationship of cooperation between entrenched
Crusaders and local peoples, but had more often
been the occasion for great brutality.

As Ayyubid rule declined and fell, in the mid-
thirteenth century Syria suffered even greater
violence at the hands of Mongol invaders: they
slaughtered fifty thousand people when they sacked
Aleppo. However, the Mongols progressed only a
little farther into Syria before being defeated in 1260
at the hands of the Mamluks, the ruling military
elite that had only recently replaced the Ayyubids in
Egypt and would govern Syria for the next two and
a half centuries. The Mamluks were unique in that
they drew their rulers only from slave-soldiers of
Turkish and Circassian origin; membership of this
military slave corps was a prerequisite for gaining
power (to prevent any ruler establishing a
hereditary dynasty). After so many centuries of
destabilizing invasions and counterinvasions, Syria
once again prospered under the regime of this class
of ascendant slaves, which patronized the arts and
Islamic scholarship.

Ottoman Rule 1516–1918

Syria next fell under the control of a vast empire whose capital was close by at Constantinople (modern-day Istanbul). Impressive in its extent and its longevity, the Ottoman Empire lasted from 1300 until just past the end of the First World War, and at its zenith stretched across three continents—North Africa, southeastern Europe, and western Asia. The Ottoman Turks wrested control of Syria from the Mamluks in 1516 and appointed deputies to rule its districts, or *vilayets*, but on the whole life changed very little; Syria was accustomed to being ruled by foreigners, and in any case the Ottomans left much of the previous administrative structure intact. The connection between ruler and ruled was loose: Constantinople's primary interest was in exacting sometimes crippling taxation from its holdings.

For the Ottomans, Syria was an important gateway to other conquests and to the pilgrimage to Mecca (the *hajj*)—no small matter since organizing pilgrimage caravans and guaranteeing their safety was a major source of the Ottoman sultans' legitimacy as rulers. Damascus was the point of departure for one of the two great Ottoman *hajj* caravans, and twenty to thirty thousand pilgrims might gather there at the outset. The most important centers of learning were now elsewhere, however, so intellectual and cultural life suffered.

As Ottoman strength waned from the eighteenth century on, European powers pressed their advantage through increasing interventions in the

Middle East: sending missionaries, winning trade concessions, and increasing trade. In Syria, the mercantile relationships they formed with Christians, and to some extent Jews, elevated the fortunes of these communities. Despite this fact, in the nineteenth century the overall economic situation declined due to competition from cheap European imported goods. General economic straits and the visibly increased wealth of minority groups combined to produce a few explosive episodes of violence along sectarian lines, first in 1840 and then in 1860, which only gave the European powers a further excuse to intervene in order to protect the scapegoated minorities. It would be only a few decades before the First World War dealt a deathblow to the Ottoman Empire and provided the European countries with an opportunity to take over, almost in one fell swoop.

Brief Independence 1918–20 and French Mandate 1920–46

When the Ottoman Empire entered the First World War on Germany's side, the British responded by backing the Arab Revolt against Ottoman rule that began in the Arabian Peninsula and reached Damascus in 1918. It was led by Prince Faisal, son of Sharif Hussein of Mecca, who had engineered the alliance with the British. Faisal assumed control of Syria, with the exception of the French-controlled coastal areas, and was proclaimed king of the Syrian Arab Kingdom. Great Power politics were too much

for him, however, since the secret Sykes-Picot Agreement between Britain and France of 1916 had already carved the region into spheres of influence for the colonial powers. Syria had been promised to France, which refused to recognize the country's

declared independence. Instead, just one month after Faisal's coronation in March 1920, France obtained a League of Nations mandate over Greater Syria, then by July had invaded and conquered the territory. Within the space of a few months, Syria had gone from being ruled by Arabs for the first time in centuries to being administered by yet another foreign power.

Once firmly established in Syria, France pursued divide-and-rule tactics that sliced the country into a series of statelets: the coastal strip that became modern-day Lebanon; Jabal al-Arab in the south; one centered on Damascus; another on Aleppo; yet another on coastal Latakia; and northern Alexandretta, later ceded to Turkey against Syria's will. With the exception of the first and last, however, these divisions failed to take hold, as the bonds between communities in Syria proved stronger than the sectarian and regional differences the French were counting on.

France was an experienced colonial power that exercised strict, heavy-handed, and thorough control. In 1925, resentment of its tactics boiled over in a revolt led by Sultan al-Atrash that began in the southern mountains and spread across Syria;

the French resorted to brutal tactics, including the systematic bombing of the civilian population of Damascus, before the conflagration was suppressed in 1927. Subsequent efforts toward independence were made by nationalist urban politicians rather than warriors, supported by strikes by the general population. Although the Free French government during the Second World War promised independence to Syria, it was only after continued political machinations—the French wanted to enshrine their influence and privileges after independence—and military skirmishes that the French admitted defeat, recognized Syria's sovereignty, and in 1946 withdrew their last troops.

Independence 1946–70

The end of colonial rule saw the establishment of a parliamentary system that was quickly ended, in 1949, by a military coup, the first in a long series of putsches that would rock Syria over the next twenty years. In the 1950s, support for pan-Arab nationalism, led by the charismatic Egyptian President Gamal Abdul Nasser, grew rapidly and in 1958 culminated in the merging of Syria and Egypt into the United Arab Republic. Nasser did not seem to have envisioned an equal partnership, but rather the acquisition of a subservient province, so Syrian politicians quickly tired of the new arrangement—although not before Egypt had helped beef up the repressive secret-police apparatus that continues to dominate Syrian political life. The union was dissolved in 1961 by a coup in Damascus that set off another round of political instability, crowned by the 1963 takeover by military officers affiliated with the socialist Ba'ath (Renaissance) Party. For the next

seven years politics were characterized by deadly internecine struggles within this ruling clique, and the state of emergency declared at the time of the Ba'athist coup remains in force today.

Syria's relationships with most of its neighbors were fractious; it had a long-running border dispute with Israel, especially over access to the waters of the Sea of Galilee, which both sides were determined to control at any cost. As tensions grew between Israel and the Arab world and Egypt massed troops along the Israeli border, Israel launched a preemptive strike on Egypt, Jordan, and Syria. The Syrian army was ill equipped, poorly directed, and weakened by political purges of the officer corps, while the Israeli military enjoyed state-of-the-art equipment and superior strategic planning abilities. Accordingly, the Syrian army— along with its Jordanian and Egyptian allies—was easily defeated in a war that lasted a mere six days; in the process, Israel occupied the Sinai in Egypt, the Gaza Strip and the West Bank in historical Palestine, and the Golan Heights in Syria—land whose return continues to be Syria's condition for peace with Israel.

The 1967 defeat was shocking and demoralizing for the Arab world, many of whose citizens, including intellectuals, had believed the propaganda their governments spread about their military prowess and Israel's imminent fall.

Era of Hafez al-Asad 1970–2000

In 1970, the era of coup and countercoup was halted when Hafez al-Asad, the former government's minister of defense, seized power in what was officially termed not a coup but a Corrective Movement. The son of a minor notable from an impoverished village in the coastal mountains who rose through the ranks of the Air Force, he kept a firm grip on the reins of government until his death in 2000, and perhaps few modern rulers could more convincingly adopt Louis XIV's maxim *"l'état, c'est moi"* due to his close management of state affairs and the indelible mark that he left on the structure of Syrian governance. Asad continued earlier Ba'athist policies of industrial nationalization and land reform, made the state the principal actor in the economy, restructured the Ba'ath Party, built up the military and the repressive intelligence services, making them pillars of his own control, advanced his own sect, the Alawites, in government, began an intervention in Lebanon that would not be finished until years after his death, and pursued a fiercely independent foreign policy.

In 1973, Syria and Egypt launched a joint surprise attack against Israel in an effort to recover their lost territories, something neither succeeded in doing—in fact, the final cease-fire lines barely budged, as initial gains by the Syrian

and Egyptian armies were later reversed. In short, the October War ended in a draw, but all sides still claimed victory. The conflict at least partially restored a sense of national pride to Syrians and helped consolidate Asad's legitimacy as ruler.

Asad did, however, face significant challenges to his tenure a few years later with the growth of a violent opposition in the shape of the Muslim Brotherhood. This Islamist group's campaign to assassinate government officials and bomb military offices provoked a fierce retaliation from the regime. This culminated in an assault on the prison at Palmyra in 1980, in which some five hundred prisoners were killed, and then in 1982 a three-week bombardment of the town of Hama, a Muslim Brotherhood stronghold. In the process, government forces destroyed most of the town's historic Old City, failed to distinguish between civilians and militants, and left five to ten thousand, or more, dead. The attack on Hama remains a taboo subject in Syria, and membership of the banned Muslim Brotherhood is punishable by death. In 1983–84 Asad also faced a significant challenge from his brother Rifa'at, who had built up a power base of his own through thousands-strong armed "Defense Companies," but Asad prevailed and Rifa'at was exiled to France.

In foreign affairs, Asad continued his predecessors' policies of alignment with the Soviet Union until its collapse, but he never allowed himself to be made a mere pawn in the Cold War struggle. And while Syrian forces never again faced Israel in open warfare, one of Asad's key objectives was always to counter Israel's powerful regional position. The Lebanese civil war that lasted from 1975 to 1990 became at least in part a proxy war between Syria and Israel, as both countries supported key militias and sent their own troops into the struggle. Syrian soldiers remained after the war's end, and were only withdrawn after international disapproval increased in the wake of the assassination of Lebanese Prime Minister Rafiq al-Hariri in 2005.

Since his death in 2000, Asad remains a towering figure in Syria whose legacy cannot be openly discussed. While he was undoubtedly a repressive autocrat, many Syrians appreciate the fact that he brought stability to a country that some fear could have become as fractured as Lebanon, modernized many aspects of the state, and made Syria, for the first time, a serious player in regional politics.

Bashar al-Asad: 2000–present

Hafez al-Asad was succeeded by his son Bashar, a British-trained ophthalmologist and technology enthusiast whose stated commitment to reform was soon tested, first by a short-lived civil-society movement known as the Damascus Spring, which a conservative backlash quickly squelched, and then by a 2005 document called the Damascus Declaration, drawn up by prominent business-people and intellectuals, which criticized the regime for its thuggery. Despite the arrest of participants in both movements, under Bashar's rule there has been some relaxation of the general strictures on free expression.

In his first decade in power, Bashar has cautiously expanded on his father's legacy by gradually opening the economy to foreign investment, moving toward normalized relations with Lebanon, and improving the country's telecommunications infrastructure. He has maintained long-standing alliances with Iran, Hamas, and Hezbollah, the last two of which remain particularly popular with much of the Syrian populace, although he has also entered into halting and indirect peace negotiations with Israel.

Articles in the Western press that blame all of Syria's political problems on the President, and insinuate that an angry and oppressed people hates him and would rise up if given the chance, are misguided. Syrians hold a wide range of attitudes toward their President, even if they prefer not to discuss them in public. Many are indeed unhappy with the political system, but that is more because of its institutional nepotism and inefficiency than solely because of its leader—who may be the most powerful figure in the government, but is still dwarfed by the inequities of the system he inherited.

GOVERNMENT AND POLITICS
Executive Branch
While the Syrian constitution officially endows the country with a tripartite government consisting of executive, legislature, and judiciary, in reality the first of these towers over the other two. The president, as its head, has the power to promulgate laws (which must also be ratified by the parliament, something that has never really proved to be a problem), declare war, appoint the vice president

and ministers, grant amnesty, and appoint military personnel and civil servants. He may serve for an unlimited number of seven-year terms, being subject at the beginning of each to a referendum in which each citizen has the option to vote *yes* or *no* to his candidacy—and they always vote *yes* in overwhelming numbers. Unless an unprecedented threat to Syria's stability surfaces, it seems likely that Bashar al-Asad will rule for the rest of his natural life.

It is common to see photos of Bashar hanging up in shops and offices around Damascus, although this is not mandatory and often does not necessarily signal devotion. Rather, it can probably be better understood as a strategy designed to ward off political suspicion and demonstrate material compliance with the basics of the regime's rule.

Legislative Branch

Although Syria has a long stop-and-go—but at times vibrant—history of parliamentary politics dating back to 1919, the current People's Assembly was created by decree in 1971 by Hafez al-Asad. This parliament may debate relatively minor matters but has no real power to shape major policies or the direction of government, and the president is empowered to dissolve it at will. Its 250 members run for election every four years, and a certain number of seats are reserved for the officially sanctioned coalition of parties called the Progressive National Front (dominated by the Ba'ath Party), while a minority of seats are held for nonaffiliated politicians.

Judicial Branch

Syria's legal system is drawn from Ottoman legislation, French codes, and Islamic law. There are courts designated for juveniles, criminal offenses, civil matters, and economic offenses. Lower courts, called "peace courts," handle less serious crimes.

The court system has three levels, with plaintiffs able to appeal decisions from the lowest courts to the mid-level courts, and then to the Court of Cassation, the highest judicial body in the country. A High Constitutional Court also rules on electoral issues and the constitutionality of laws and decrees. Under the State of Emergency, certain defendants may be tried in Security Courts, which drop what legal safeguards are offered in the regular criminal courts and are primarily used for politically expedient goals.

Issues such as marriage, divorce, inheritance, and the custody of children are subject to personal status laws that vary according to religious affiliation, so that members of each community are bound by laws based on their own traditions and adjudicated by their own religious courts.

The Ba'ath Party

Perhaps equal in political importance to the legislative and judicial branches is the Ba'ath (Renaissance) Party itself, which has been integrated into the political system at every level, although it has largely abandoned its ideology in favor of the pragmatic exercise of power. It wasn't always this way: when the Ba'ath was founded in the 1940s by the Syrian intellectuals Michel Aflaq and Salah ad-Din al-Bitar, it was a party of pan-Arab idealism whose goal was to improve the plight of the Arabs through unity and social justice. Its role as an ideological guide slowly diminished, however, after Hafez al-Asad's decisive seizure of power, as he shaped it instead into a patronage network and pillar of control. The Ba'ath Party today is a shortcut to upward social mobility for members, an umbrella organizer of unions, and an arbiter of personnel appointments in the bureaucracy and the armed forces by way of a parallel structure of committees that oversee government and military offices. It dominates all other political parties through its legally enshrined position as a first among equals in the Progressive National Front. The Ba'ath Party in Syria shares historical roots with, but is completely separate from, Saddam Hussein's rival Ba'ath Party that was once in power in Iraq.

THE ECONOMY

In the 1960s and 1970s, the socialist dimension of Ba'ath Party doctrine pushed the government to nationalize industries, redistribute land, and take a leading role in economic planning. The state became the single largest employer, and despite the low salaries of public servants, many Syrians still covet government jobs for their ironclad security. Foreign direct investment was severely restricted, although Syria did benefit from military and economic aid from both the Gulf States and the USSR. While Hafez al-Asad undertook a few economic reforms in response to the recession of the 1980s, Bashar has taken more significant steps, such as legalizing private banking in 2001, relaxing government controls on currency, encouraging foreign investment, lifting some price subsidies, and opening the Damascus Securities Exchange in 2009. Nonetheless, economic liberalization is slow, wages are low, unemployment is high—while the economic relaxation thus far has provided more opportunities for those well-placed to take advantage of them, it certainly hasn't lifted all equally—and Syria's growing young population will require yet more jobs as it joins the workforce.

Agriculture has long been a mainstay of Syria's economy, and though its relative importance is declining, it still employs around 20 percent of the labor force and produces food for export; the chief agricultural products are cotton, wheat, barley, and fruits and vegetables. State-run irrigation projects have increased the amount of arable land to about a third of the country's area, and achieved agricultural self-sufficiency in many crops.

Syria has drilled low-quality oil since the 1960s, and in the 1980s discovered significant reserves of high-quality oil in the Euphrates valley; ever since then, the export of this oil has accounted for a significant, but decreasing, part of the state budget. Production peaked in the 1990s, domestic demand is growing, and Syria's reserves are expected to continue to decline in the coming years.

Tourism plays an increasingly important role

in Syria's economy, as the government looks to this sector to offset dwindling oil revenues and has encouraged investment in the country's tourism infrastructure; a slightly rosier international image hasn't hurt, either. Tourism now accounts for more than 10 percent of the country's GDP, and officials hope that proportion will continue to rise.

SYRIA AND THE WORLD

After years of diplomatic isolation, Syria is emerging from the cold, enjoying new trade agreements with Europe, and in 2010 the appointment of an American ambassador to Damascus (after the post had gone unfilled for five years, a diplomatic slap on the wrist for Syria's alleged role in the assassination of Lebanese Prime Minister Rafiq al-Hariri). Its government is seen as a key Middle Eastern player, and is looked to as a major part of any possible comprehensive Middle Eastern peace deal. Syria has also normalized its relationship with Lebanon and formed a new, close relationship with Turkey, once an adversary. Additionally, Damascus has pragmatically continued its decades-old alliance with Iran and its support for Hamas and Hezbollah—part of a long-standing commitment to resisting Israeli regional dominance. Syria and Israel, having never signed a peace agreement, remain officially at war; their occasional indirect negotiations have never borne fruit. But with the exception of this southern neighbor, Syria in many ways is one of the popular new kids at school, with enough friends to count on for the time being, and enough patience to see which ones will last.

chapter two

VALUES & ATTITUDES

PAN-ARAB PRIDE

The official ideology of the governing Syrian Ba'ath Party is that of Arab nationalism, holding that all Arab countries are one nation at heart and that unity is the way to an Arab revival. However, it's more than mere government rhetoric: Syrians are deeply proud of their Arab heritage, its local Syrian expressions, and the Arabic language. While most other Arab countries teach university-level science classes in English or French, Syria stubbornly asserts that the Arabic language is just as useful for such subjects as any other, translating all necessary textbooks into Arabic.

Similarly, Syrian education emphasizes an appreciation of the Arabic poetic tradition. When an American and a Syrian student riding a public bus together in Damascus got into a friendly but loud argument over the authorship of a famous classical Arabic poem, the American was surprised to find his fellow passengers jumping into the fracas: not only did they know who had written the poem, they had long passages memorized as well!

Being Arab can be as important as being Syrian: the word for foreigners, *ajaanib*, is applied to Westerners, Africans, Asians, South Americans, and the like—but not to citizens of other Arab countries, who aren't quite foreign, but rather something closer to home.

Arabism and the Palestinian Struggle

Sympathy with the Palestinian people is widespread
in Syria, and extends to solidarity with Hezbollah
(in southern Lebanon) and Hamas (in Gaza),
groups that Syrians see as carrying on a legitimate
political struggle against Israel. While the Western
press and governments often
characterize Hamas and
Hezbollah as terrorist
organizations, Syrians disagree,
instead viewing groups such as
al-Qaeda on the one hand, and
occupying armies on the other,
as the real terrorists. In keeping
with pan-Arab sentiment, the
former president, Hafez al-Asad,
made containing Israeli power a
cornerstone of his foreign
policy—although he was also

keen to keep the Palestinians' struggle operating on
his terms, not their own. In a continuation of his
policies, the Syrian government still maintains close
ties with groups like Hamas and Hezbollah, and
casts itself as an advocate of justice in Palestine.

SOCIAL AND PERSONAL RELATIONSHIPS

Political attitudes aren't everything, of course: in
day-to-day life, Syrians place a high value on their
relationships with friends and family. Hospitality is
taken very seriously, and treating guests badly—
which includes not offering them enough to eat!—
is considered a major breach of etiquette. Family
harmony is more important than individual
satisfaction, and good relationships are more

important than ambition. Equally key are friendliness, good manners, and a willingness to help others out.

Respect for authority figures, such as teachers, parents, and the elderly, is crucial. Syrians might kiss their parents' hands, for example, in order to show love and deference, and they'll stand so that an older person can find a seat on the bus. Hierarchies also determine who has the ultimate say in decision making: just as elders expect the young to obey them, men expect to be deferred to by women.

"CUSTOMS AND TRADITIONS"

Not all values are the subject of universal agreement: conservative Syrians love it when people adhere to the *a'adaat wa taqaleed,* or "customs and traditions." This is an oft-repeated phrase that can be used to justify any kind of social habit that's not necessarily enshrined in religion, or to emphasize the importance of doing things the way one's forefathers did (quite selectively, though—one doesn't hear that the *a'adaat wa taqaleed* prohibit cell phones or television, but they may keep girls from going out alone at night). Others see the same traditions as shackles to be thrown off— like the famous Syrian poet Adonis (the nom de plume of Ali Ahmed Said), who called for a cultural rupture and break with the past.

WORK AND LEISURE

The fact that many things progress slowly in Syria can fool visitors into thinking that Syrians do not work very hard. In fact, many take two jobs or work very long hours just to support their families—a necessity due to low wages, rising prices, and the inefficiencies that make it difficult to achieve much in a short period of time. Nonetheless, Syrians make the most of this situation and approach it with good humor: even a taxi driver working twelve-hour days is eager to have a pleasant conversation with his passenger, and a shopkeeper who sits behind his counter just as long still greets customers with a smile. The purpose of all this extra work, however, is to provide for one's family, not to work for its own sake, since investing time in family and friends is very important—and being busy with work isn't an adequate excuse not to.

A SENSE OF UNFAIRNESS

The great tradition of Syrian hospitality and openness to Arabs and foreigners alike—a willingness to welcome them into their country and often their homes—stands in stark contrast to the prevalence of borders in Syrian life, claustrophobically close by and excruciatingly difficult to cross. Syrians may easily travel to Turkey, Jordan, and Lebanon, but the wider world—in particular the West—is unwelcoming to ordinary Syrian passport holders. Any visa application to study or work in North America or Europe is a reminder of those enormous forces in world politics against which individuals are powerless, but which nonetheless exert an outsize influence on their lives. Syrians who fill out detailed paperwork and wait months to find out whether or not they've been granted foreign visas are often greeted in the end with the same news: no, you may not cross our border.

STATUS AND CLASS

Syria has long been a center of commerce for both the ancient and modern worlds, so its urban elites were traditionally religious or commercial, with inherited wealth and status, while rural notables and landowners dominated the countryside as part of a semifeudal structure that kept the peasantry in various degrees of subjugation.

The ruling Ba'ath Party's rise to power in the 1960s with its economic reforms—nationalization of industries and land redistribution—put an end to feudalism and reduced the power of the old mercantile ruling class. In its place, a new political elite centered on the army and party leadership arose, mostly drawn from the coastal mountain peasantry whose ascendance had begun with French policies that made religious minorities the backbone of the colonial army; it was solidified though Ba'ath dominance in the 1960s and Hafez al-Asad's firm grip on power thereafter.

As the opening up of the economy progressed cautiously in the 1990s and more quickly after 2000, a new economic elite rose out of the beneficiaries of privatization and international trade, often drawn from those in the old elites who were best-placed to take advantage of such ventures. The availability of foreign goods has made conspicuous consumption ever more important as a status marker, although it has certainly not reached the same degree of intensity as in nearby Beirut. To some degree, the importance of wealth has surpassed that of inherited family prestige as a marker of social status. The middle class includes small-time merchants and businessmen, civil servants, and those who have entered into prestigious occupations like medicine, engineering, law, and university professorship by way of the educational system. Syrian cities, regions, and religious groups also contain their own sub-elites, who wield local political and economic power.

AN URBANIZED COUNTRY, WITH RURAL TIES

In the mid-twentieth century new farming techniques and a growing population led to a rapid increase in urbanization that shaped the development of Syria's cities. The existing housing infrastructure was frequently unable to support so many migrants, so newcomers built their own accommodation on the urban outskirts in settlements that later gained official sanction and government services. Rural migrants usually moved in close to the friends and family who'd come before them, so many urban areas mimic whole regions of Syria in their economic and religious composition. These migrants visit their villages and towns of origin frequently for holidays, funerals, and vacations, maintaining close ties that make these areas the site of their primary regional allegiance, rather than the city where their family may have lived for decades. Villages are seen as being more beautiful, pure, and wholesome than the crowded and dirty cities, but poor places to find work: economic activity in the country focuses on agriculture, which employs a decreasing percentage of the population. Conservatism is found in Syrian cities and rural areas alike, but the cities have a cosmopolitanism not present in the countryside.

SOCIAL NETWORKS

The best—and sometimes only—way to get something done in Syria is by way of *wasta*, the system of personal connections sometimes referred to as "Vitamin Wow" with the kind of resigned derision one directs toward a particularly unpleasant family member, someone whom you've learned to live with since it's not clear you could ever rid yourself of them. *Wasta* is a form of social capital that comes from mobilizing friendships and family relationships for reciprocal favors. It can be used to find jobs for yourself or your children, to win a place at a coveted department in a university, to speed up a lengthy government procedure, to get high-speed Internet installed in your home, to have a court case dismissed, or to gain any other of life's necessities and extravagances. Anyone who performs these sorts of favors for their friends and family expects to be repaid with similar services later on.

This kind of social networking ossifies existing inequalities, helping the rich and well-connected grow more so while minimizing the value of a university education which—without *wasta*—can be insufficient for entry into a graduate's chosen field. Syrians detest the role of *wasta*, but for an individual to forsake it would mean living a life of deprivation without significantly impacting the system.

RELIGION

Syrians of any religion typically value piety— although it's certainly possible to find Syrian atheists and agnostics as well—and the past few decades have seen a rise in public expressions of religious observance, a trend that mirrors the wider

Middle East. Most obviously, the number of urban women who don the *hijab* has risen sharply during this period. However, it's still rude to question others about their personal religious beliefs before you know them well.

A Note on Sectarianism and Secularism

Sectarianism is one of the specters that haunt Syrian government—something that's understandable in a country with so many potentially divisive ethnic and religious affiliations. In neighboring Lebanon, these divisions helped mobilize the forces of a bloody fifteen-year civil war. Hence, not only is drawing direct attention to sectarian differences impolite, it can be politically dangerous. In conversation, regional affiliations can stand in for religious ones in order to avoid making overt reference to faith—for example, someone who refers to "the people of as-Suwayda" is usually talking about the Druze.

Syria's government is officially secular, with caveats: the president must be a Muslim; Islamic law is one source of national law; each religious group has its own personal status laws governing marriage, divorce, and inheritance; and members of the president's own sect, the Alawites, enjoy an unofficial preference in the army and security service. It's a delicate balance, but one that is at least functional: while some Syrians may express religious bigotry in personal conversations, such opinions are confined to the private sphere and interfaith relations are good on an official level—just as many Syrians are genuinely tolerant even in their private lives.

Sunni Islam

The origins of Islam, the faith now professed by a quarter of the world's population, go back to the year 610 CE in the Arabian Peninsula when the Prophet Muhammad, fasting in a cave, heard a voice commanding him: "Recite!" He did so, and what emerged miraculously from his mouth were the verses of the *Qur'an*, revealed over the next few decades and compiled in a book after his death. Over the same period of time, Muhammad proceeded to establish the earthly foundations of the nascent religion, leading a small community of followers in the cities of Medina and Mecca in modern-day Saudi Arabia that remain holy for Muslims. Like other key religious-historical figures, Muhammad was a social reformer in addition to being a religious leader: he asked his followers to give up idol worship, infanticide, and alcohol; called on them to provide for poorer members of the community; and allowed women to inherit property. His core theological claim, made in a social milieu in which many gods were worshipped, was the absolute unity of one God, who spoke directly to mankind through the *Qur'an.*

Islam was deeply changed and diversified in the process of its enormous growth over the following fourteen centuries. During Muhammad's lifetime, his judgments and the direct revelation of the *Qur'an* were sufficient to solve the dilemmas that arose; since that time, a body of law governing Muslim societies has developed to deal with the same kinds of issues in the absence of such direct guidance. Called *shari'a,* it is a complex set of overlapping religious rulings and legal decisions that cover all aspects of life, from politics and economics to hygiene, loosely grouped into four schools of law. Syrians usually follow the Hanafi school.

Stories and anecdotes about Muhammad's life called the *hadith* help guide Sunni Muslims—a majority of Muslims worldwide—in the practical aspects of a pious life, and form a source of Sunni Islamic law.

From the time of Muhammad's death until less than a century ago, temporal Islamic authority was embodied in the person of a caliph, supposedly the worldly leader of the Muslim community even though Islam had quickly grown too large to realistically be united under a single leader. The position was abolished in 1924 by the Turkish president Mustafa Kemal Attaturk, and no one has managed to revive it since. In terms of religious authority, Sunni Islam does not have a formal clerical hierarchy: any Muslim man can lead his community in prayer, and any Muslim scholar can issue a *fatwa*, or Islamic legal ruling. As a result, there are often conflicting *fatwas* on the same subject. Naturally, some Islamic scholars have more influence than others, and some *fatwas*—which are not binding in any case—are more widely obeyed than others.

Muslims revere Muhammad as the greatest prophet and an exemplary human being, but he is entirely human, not divine; nor is he considered to be the author of the *Qur'an*. Instead, this holy book is believed to be the literal word of God, delivered directly through the speech of a man. Incidentally, the word "Allah" in Arabic just means "the God," and does not refer specifically to a "Muslim God";

all Arabic speakers, whether or not they are
Muslim, indicate God using this word. Muslims see
Islam as the completion of and complement to
Christianity and Judaism, and they hail Abraham,
Moses, Jesus, and other Judeo-Christian figures as
prophets who revealed part of God's word, albeit in
imperfect form. Similarly, the *Qur'an* contains
many of the same stories as the Bible and the Torah.

THE FIVE PILLARS OF ISLAM

Observant Muslims try to follow the "five
pillars of Islam," or the five most important
aspects of piety:

- The profession of faith, stating that "there is
  no god but God and Muhammad is the
  prophet of God."
- At least one pilgrimage to Mecca for those
  who are physically and financially able.
- A yearly tithe called *zakaat*, a percentage of
  one's income given to the poor.
- Fasting during the holy month of Ramadan.
- Prayer five times daily. The call to prayer,
  called the *azaan*, is audible in most parts of
  Syria as it signals the prayers: just before
  sunrise, at noon, in the late afternoon, at
  sunset, and in the evening. The only prayer
  that must be performed in the mosque is the
  noon prayer on Fridays, which is a time for
  communities to come together in worship.

Shia' Islam

Some theological differences between Shi'ite and
Sunni Muslims have developed over the last

millennium and a half, though initially they were solely political. Shi'ites were originally the faction of the first Muslims who believed that leadership of the Muslim community should only be held by members of the Prophet's own family. The definitive historical event for Shia' Islam was the battle of Karbala (in modern-day Iraq), in which the Umayyad Caliph Yazid slaughtered the woefully outnumbered troops that the Prophet's relative Hussein led against him—a feat made much easier by the fact that Hussein's allies at Kufa failed to come to his aid. Shia' Islam grew out of the penance rituals that developed to commemorate Hussein's self-sacrifice and to bemoan his followers' desertion.

The Shia' differ from the Sunnis in their belief in a lineage of divinely inspired imams, or leaders, descended from the Prophet Muhammad through his cousin and son-in-law Ali. In fact, the term "Shia'" is derived from *Shia'tu 'Ali* (the Party of Ali). Different Shia' sects revere a different number of imams: a majority of Shia' Muslims are "Twelvers," who believe in twelve imams (the last of whom, the Mehdi, is said to be waiting in Occultation until he returns on the Day of Judgment), while Isma'ilis acknowledge only seven. Shia' Muslims also have their own school of Islamic law that is defined by the rulings of a complex hierarchy of religious scholars and draws on sources not acknowledged by Sunni religious authorities.

Alawites

The Alawites are a sect of Shia' Islam, once considered heretical but now more widely accepted, who have historically lived in Syria's coastal mountains in poverty and isolation. Their fortunes began to change due to French preferential policies, and their rise was bolstered by the ascendance of one of their own sons to the presidency. The Alawite religion is highly secretive, and only initiates are allowed to know its details, but in general it seems to include a reverence of both Muhammad and the *Qur'an* in addition to other secret texts, belief in reincarnation, the divinity of Ali, the origin of their people as literal stars, and the authority of twelve imams after Muhammad. The hidden nature of their beliefs means that, for the majority of Syrian Alawites who are not initiates, everyday religious practice is determined by custom, not texts. Alawites form about 13 percent of Syria's population.

Druze

The Druze people are just as friendly as their religion is exclusive and enigmatic, its secrets revealed only to a tiny group of initiates, and its syncretic beliefs not entirely clear. The Druze share some tenets of faith with Isma'ili Shiism, from which they diverged in the eleventh century. No one can convert in or out of the religion, and intermarriage with other sects or religions is prohibited, although it occurs in practice. The Druze form about 3 percent of Syria's population and live mainly in the Golan Heights, Idleb, and the southern Jabal al-Arab, where they migrated in the eighteenth and nineteenth centuries from Mount Lebanon. That their community produced the initial spark and leadership for the 1925 revolution against French rule in Syria is a source of continuing pride for today's Syrian Druze.

Christianity

Christians have been present in small numbers in Syria almost from the religion's earliest days, although it wasn't until perhaps the mid-fourth century in Damascus, and later for rural areas, that Christians became a majority in the country. This ubiquity, of course, later gave way to the slow spread of Islam through the population in the centuries following the Arab invasion of 640. During the fifth century Christianity was riven by disputes over the nature of Christ—was he both human and divine, divine *only,* or some complex combination of the two?—and the numerous church entities resulting from these arguments still survive, peaceably, in Syria's multiplicity of Christian sects.

While a majority of Christians adhere to the Greek Orthodox (also called Melkite) Church, there are also Syrian Christians who are Nestorians, Chaldean Catholics, Assyrian Orthodox, Assyrian Catholics, Armenian Orthodox, Armenian Catholics, Maronites, Greek Catholics, Syriac Orthodox, Syriac Catholics, Protestants, and Roman Catholics (the last two grew out of European missionary activities). The Churches designated "Catholic" are thus named because they accept the authority of Rome, but preserve their own traditions and liturgy. The relationship between Christian sects is generally good.

Syrian Christians are more likely to be urban, well educated, materially well-off, and to have studied in private schools than their non-Christian counterparts, an outgrowth of the close and beneficial relationships dating back centuries between Christian communities and European businessmen and missionaries. However, they are also culturally Arab (some of the early Arab nationalist leaders in Syria were Christian) and don't tend to differ from the population at large in their political opinions—although they may appreciate more deeply the Syrian government's official secularism and its overall evenhanded approach to religious minorities.

Jews

The Jewish population in Syria was once some thirty thousand strong, the legacy of communities that had lived in the area for millennia and of Jews who found safe haven all over the Middle East after their expulsion from Spain in 1492. Although many left Syria during the first half of the nineteenth century to pursue better economic prospects in the USA and Europe, the largest exodus followed the explosion of anti-Jewish suspicion and violence provoked by the UN plan for the partition of Palestine in 1947 and the establishment of the state of Israel in 1948. The Jews who remained in Syria faced severe restrictions on internal movement, emigration, and commerce, which President Hafez al-Asad later eased somewhat; most of the rest of the community emigrated when he lifted the travel ban completely in 1992. Currently fewer than two hundred Jews, mainly elderly, live in Syria, the bulk of them in Damascus, while the largest community of Syrian Jews is currently found in New York.

Anti-Israeli feeling runs high in Syria. Many Syrians recognize the difference between Israelis and Jews, but since plenty of others do not, Jewish visitors would be wise not to divulge their religion except to those whom they trust. An equally good reason for Jews not to broadcast their religion in Syria is the scrutiny to which the state security services sometimes subject known Jewish visitors.

ETHNIC AND POLITICAL MINORITIES
Kurds

The Kurds are a stateless ethnic group spread across Syria, Turkey, Iran, and Iraq. Although their ethnic origins are uncertain, their language is related to Persian. Mainly Sunni Muslims, they are thought to compose around 9 percent of Syria's population and are concentrated in urban areas and the northeastern plains. Some Kurds have been highly integrated into the Arab population, taking on Arabic names and losing their Kurdish language skills, while others speak primarily Kurdish within their communities and consider themselves as more Kurdish than Syrian. Any expression of a Kurdish political identity or demands for an independent state are viewed by the central government as a threat—but expressions of Kurdish culture are now more accepted than in the past. In 1962, the central government stripped about 120,000 Kurds of their Syrian citizenship, claiming that they were not genuine Syrians but "alien infiltrators" who had entered the country illicitly. These men and women and their descendants are undocumented; they work in the informal economy and don't enjoy the same rights as other Syrians to education and health care.

Smaller Ethnic Minorities

Syria is also home to about 150,000 Armenians, who found refuge in Syria from the Armenian Genocide (1915–18, 1920–23) and live mainly in Aleppo. There are also smaller populations of Assyrians, an Aramaic-speaking people indigenous to the Middle East, and Turkmen, a Turkic people originally from Central Asia.

The Palestinian Refugee Population

Some 460,000 or more Palestinian refugees from the 1948 and 1967 wars currently reside in Syria, a large number in a suburb of Damascus and many of the rest in refugee camps that dot the country and have long since assumed the aspect of dense urban neighborhoods rather than the flimsy, impermanent tent-towns they once were. Syria's pan-Arabism is put to work in the service of these refugees, granting them most of the same rights as Syrians to education and health care and meaning that they enjoy better conditions than the Palestinians in many other Arab countries. They're not citizens, however, and carry travel documents, not passports—another ideological move, since granting Palestinians citizenship would mean that they were envisaged to be staying in the country forever.

Palestinians appreciate the haven they've found in Syria, but view it as a temporary stop on the way to the ultimate goal of their return to Palestine. Ask a Palestinian person born in Syria where he or she is from, and you'll be told the name of a grandfather's village or city in Palestine—and in a Palestinian accent, not a Syrian one.

The Iraqi Refugee Population

The US-led invasion of Iraq in 2003 led to the displacement of several million Iraqis, some 1.2–1.5 million of whom entered Syria (often of lower social status than the upper middle-class refugees who preferred Jordan). The vast majority have settled around the outskirts of Damascus. Initially, it was easy for Iraqi refugees to pour into the country. In accordance with its Arab nationalist ideology, in the past Syria did not normally require citizens of Arab countries to obtain visas beforehand for visits, or limit the duration of their stay; visas were automatically granted and renewed. In October 2007, however, the government began to require Iraqis to obtain visas prior to entering the country. Iraqis may attend Syrian schools through the secondary level, but cannot work legally, although on a practical level they (like many Syrians) find employment in the informal economy; for health care, food assistance, and other basic services they rely on themselves and on the UN High Commissioner for Refugees, the Syrian Red Crescent, and other nongovernmental organizations (NGOs).

Iraqi refugees generally have no attachment to Syria, and are eager either to be repatriated or to be resettled abroad. Resettlement is slow and only obtained by a tiny minority of refugees, so, while violence in Iraq has not entirely abated, some who've exhausted their means in Syria are choosing to return to their homeland. Officially Iraqis are welcomed in Syria to an extraordinary degree, but they are regarded with suspicion by some Syrians, who believe that their presence has contributed to the rapid price rise of basic commodities and real estate over the last few years, and associate the areas they live in with poverty and higher crime rates.

ATTITUDES TOWARD WOMEN

Women are highly visible in some aspects of the public sphere, and becoming more so all the time: they attend college in large numbers and work outside the home in a wide range of professions, from teaching to medicine to engineering and more. One of Syria's two current vice presidents, Dr. Najah al-Attar, is female. Women enjoy most of the legal rights that men do, though Syrian society is very patriarchal and women continue to face a number of cultural barriers, such as a severe double standard in terms of social and sexual behavior and an expectation that family should be their first priority, so that even working women are burdened with the full second job of tending their children and their homes. Syria might be said to occupy the middle ground in the spectrum of Middle Eastern countries: it's more socially conservative than its neighbors Lebanon and Turkey, but more liberal than many other Arab nations, and sexual harassment exists at much lower levels than in countries like Egypt.

A Note on Women's Clothing

In keeping with the patriarchal tradition of judging women mostly on their appearance, in the West considerable significance is often placed on how Muslim and Arab women dress, which implies a belief in a one-to-one correlation between a woman's clothing and her character or her beliefs. This is, of course, erroneous. Syrian women have myriad reasons for their choice of dress, which ranges from the very scanty in certain nightclubs to being entirely covered. Women who wear a scarf over their hair may do so because of personal conviction, familial or social pressures, economic necessity (if she can't afford to spend much money on her looks), or a variety of other reasons. Not all Muslim women cover their hair, and there are large variations in style among those who do.

A note on vocabulary is also in order: a *hijab* is a piece of cloth that covers the hair, while the *niqab* is a black covering for the face (or most of it); an *abaya* is a long, black, decorated robe worn over clothing,  and a *manteau* is a plain, ankle-length jacket. The *burka*, a one-piece garment covering the wearer from head to toe, with a mesh over the eyes, is worn in Afghanistan, never in Syria, and the *chador* is a piece of black cloth wrapped around the head and body worn primarily by Iranians (who can be observed on pilgrimage in Syria).

In public, the minimum modest dress for Syrian women means clothing covering their legs, shoulders, cleavage, and entire stomachs and backs, so shirts that part with your jeans when you lean over are not advised! For Syrian girls, clothes that cover these areas can be considered modest enough even if they're worn skintight—and they often are. Foreign women would do well to bear in mind that standards of dress are not uniform across cities and regions, and when in doubt, dressing more conservatively will never be problematic, but showing too much skin can attract unwanted attention.

ATTITUDES TOWARD HOMOSEXUALS

In Syria homosexuality exists in underground circles, but it is not accepted by the public at large, even in more educated and liberal society. Gay visitors would do well to be cautious in disclosing this aspect of their identity to Syrians, as only a small minority is comfortable with the notion. Not all Syrian men who sleep with other men would be willing to call themselves "gay" at all, since they view such behavior as a practice and not an identity.

HONOR AND REPUTATION

Honor and reputation are defined not only by individual behavior but also through that of one's family members: a woman whose honor is damaged hurts not only her own marriage prospects, but those of her sisters as well. For women, honor and reputation are defined by chastity: they are expected to be virgins when they marry. Beforehand they should not even have entered into any situation in which they *might* have lost their virginity: spending time with a man alone behind closed doors, for example, or sleeping away from home. For men, honor is defined primarily by their ability to exercise control over the women in their family, specifically enforcing their chastity and keeping them out of any circumstances that could throw it into doubt. In a looser sense, reputation can refer to a family's background, professional status, and wealth.

In the worst cases, doubts about a woman's chastity can result in "honor crimes," in which a family, in order to cleanse its honor, murders a female relative suspected of sexual activity. Although Syria recently raised the minimum prison sentence for these crimes, at only two years it remains quite low. Honor crimes are not in fact terribly common; rather, they are the tip of the craggy iceberg of the notion of honor, whose repercussions are ordinarily far less dire. The list of behaviors that are considered impermissible for women—that is, considered potentially to cast doubt on their honor—varies from family to family and community to community. Some believe that girls shouldn't have any social contact with unrelated men before marriage; for others, cross-gender friendships are fine but dating is not; some might not mind dating as long as it's restricted to sitting in cafés and restaurants. This is not to say that Syrian women adhere, sheeplike, to these boundaries—quite a lot of rule bending and evasion is less the exception than the norm.

POLITICAL SENSITIVITY AND FREEDOM OF SPEECH

Some articles in the Western press have portrayed Syria as a totalitarian state that tolerates no dissent, but this one-sided picture is quite far from the truth. There are a few "third rails" of political speech in Syria that should never be touched in public, first among which is the performance of the current president and his father, but also including topics such as sectarian differences and politics, the history and repression of Islamic extremism, and the repressive tactics of the security forces. There is much that *can* be said, however: government policies, corruption, and bureaucracy may be critiqued if the criticisms are directed at lower-level officials and don't implicate the highest echelons of government.

The degree of freedom of speech that each individual enjoys depends not only on *what* is being said, but on *who* is saying it, and *to whom*: those with powerful family and friends can criticize with relative ease, while the poorly connected must be reticent. A politically sensitive statement that might not elicit any official reaction—or even be noticed—when penned by an unknown, little-read blogger could provoke a backlash if written by a well-known dissident. Although the government does ban books, bookstore owners often stock these behind the counter, while banned Web sites are even more easily and frequently accessed. The point, after all, is less to keep *anyone* from accessing these products or criticizing the government, but to keep much of this criticism within limited, fragmented, disorganized circles. Foreigners would do well to respect the political sensitivities of Syrians, and let their Syrian friends who feel comfortable doing so bring up any politically sensitive topics themselves.

ATTITUDES TOWARD THE LAW

Laws in Syria are pliable, vague, and rarely applied consistently. Exceptions can be made, according to who is involved and how much government officials stand to gain from it. For example, satellite dishes were banned in Syria throughout the 1990s, but they spread across many rooftops anyway because a high-level government official profited from importing them! The same goes for plenty of laws and policies.

Getting Ahead

An American businesswoman working in Syria was riding in a taxi, when she noticed that the driver was driving in the middle of the road, directly over the painted dividing line between the lanes.

"Why are you driving like that?" she asked him.

"It's faster this way," he answered.

And so it is with many things in Syria: the one who follows the law in all its details loses, while those who take shortcuts can get ahead, even if only a little.

MULTILAYERED IDENTITY

As we have seen, identity in Syria is multifaceted. Individual Syrians incorporate their gender, religion, sect, ethnicity, socioeconomic status, plus multiple regional affiliations that can extend to units as small as the neighborhood they grew up in and over areas as large as the Arab world. Ascribing a Syrian's values to any one aspect of their identity would certainly mean doing them an injustice— and, on a larger scale, it would remove much of what's unique and fascinating about the country.

CUSTOMS & TRADITIONS

CALENDARS

Daily life in Syria runs on the Western, Gregorian calendar, but the normal workweek is Sunday to Thursday with a Friday–Saturday weekend. Observant Muslim men attend noon prayers at mosques on Fridays, but Christians may take the morning off on Sundays in order to attend their own services. Some newspapers and books also note the date according to the Islamic calendar, whose first year fell in 622 CE, when the Prophet Muhammad traveled from the city of Mecca to Medina with his followers, establishing the foundations of the first Muslim community. The Islamic calendar is lunar, so on the Gregorian calendar religious holidays are celebrated eleven days earlier each year. Furthermore, while Catholics in Syria calculate the dates of their holidays according to the Gregorian calendar, Orthodox communities use the Julian calendar, meaning that the two communities' celebrations of Easter can fall weeks apart. Kurds, though mainly Sunni Muslims, also calculate their own non-Muslim holidays using an Iranian solar calendar that dates from 612 BCE and begins on the spring equinox (though it is not used in daily life).

MAJOR RELIGIOUS HOLIDAYS
Ramadan and Eid al-Fitr

Perhaps the best-known of the Muslim holidays, Ramadan is the yearly lunar month of fasting during which observant Muslims abstain, from dawn until dusk, from eating, drinking, smoking, and sex, in commemoration of the Islamic month in which the *Qur'an* was first revealed to the Prophet Muhammad. Dates vary according to the lunar calendar. Although it's now possible to calculate the exact beginning and ending of the lunar months, Syria, like many Muslim-majority countries, preserves the tradition of assigning a committee to observe the moon visually before declaring an official start to Ramadan—meaning that different countries often begin and end their fasting on different days. Ramadan is a time for families and the Muslim community to come together as they awake before dawn each day to eat *suhuur,* the meal that must sustain them throughout the day, then join together again after sundown for the fast-breaking meal of *iftar.* It's also a time to reflect on God, religious duties, piety, self-control, and the plight of the poor, whom organizations and wealthy individuals remember with free public *iftars.*

Ramadan is as steeped in cultural traditions as it is in religious significance: certain foods and drinks are cooked and sold specially for the holiday, such as *tamr hindi* (tamarind juice), *qamr ad-diin* (apricot juice), and deserts like *qtayaf,* sweet dough pockets filled with nuts and cheese. Many of the television serials that have been under production all year in Syria are first broadcast during this time, with new episodes aired every evening of the holy month. Businesses reduce their daytime working hours, and activity in predominantly Muslim areas halts almost completely just before sundown, when shopkeepers and businesspeople rush home for *iftar,* then open up again after the meal. In the dark of the early morning, a *musahharati* (a neighborhood drummer and caller) visits some areas, beating a drum and crying out loudly in order to wake residents for the predawn meal. Muslims also attend special post-*iftar* prayers, called *taraweeh,* in which they recite a portion of the *Qur'an,* allowing them to have completed the entire book by the end of the month.

Non-Muslims in Syria, and Muslims who have chosen not to fast, are expected to respect their fellow citizens' religious observances by refraining from eating or drinking in front of them or on the street; Muslims who are sick or traveling, or women who are pregnant or menstruating, may also eat discreetly during the day, although they compensate for these days by fasting when they're able later in the year.

The end of Ramadan is marked by the celebration of the three-day Eid al-Fitr, or the Feast of the Breaking of the Fast, and many Syrians who have moved away from their villages of origin visit them on these days. On the first and most important day of the holiday, men and boys rise early to attend a special prayer service in the mosque before returning home to participate in the extensive visits to family and friends that will take place throughout the holiday. Everyone is expected to wear something new, so parents often give their children gifts of new outfits, and adults either wear new attire or pull out the best from their existing wardrobe. Women adorn themselves with rarely worn jewelry. Despite the rise in prices during Ramadan and the final rush to purchase new garb, the holiday is not yet heavily commercialized. Rather, it is dedicated to reflection and to enjoying the food and drink that the observant have denied themselves by day, consumed in the presence of good company.

Eid al-Adha

Eid al-Adha is the other major Islamic holiday of the year for Sunni Muslims; its dates also vary. This Feast of the Sacrifice commemorates the obedience that the biblical and Qur'anic Abraham—whom Islam considers an important prophet—displayed to God when he prepared to sacrifice his son (Ishmael, not Isaac as in the Bible) on God's command; impressed by such piety, God provided Abraham with a ram to sacrifice instead. The modern Eid al-Adha is a four-day holiday that provides an occasion to reflect on such obedience, which Muslims symbolically reenact by sacrificing an animal (usually a sheep), then distributing its meat to the poor. It's also a time to conduct extensive visits with family and friends.

Eid al-Adha also marks the end of the period of *hajj,* or pilgrimage to Mecca, a religious duty that all Muslims who are financially and bodily able must perform at least once in their lives. A pilgrimage to Mecca is known as *hajj* only if it is made during this precise time of year, the four days in the twelfth

Islamic month that precedes Eid al-Adha. During any other time of year, a pilgrimage to Mecca is called *'omra*, a "minor pilgrimage" that isn't mandatory for Muslims but is nonetheless a devout act. Both *hajj* and *'omra* include similar acts of piety designed to reenact scenes from the life of Abraham and other events in sacred history. The *hajj* itself is a deeply meaningful experience of communal worship and purification for all who perform it.

Christmas

Some Syrian Christians, especially those who observe Eastern rites, begin the celebration of Christmas by fasting for Advent, which entails abstaining from meat and dairy products on certain days; they also decorate the outside of their apartments with lights and adorn trees inside. On Christmas Eve, Christians attend church in the evening and share a meal afterward; the celebration usually spills onto the streets, with numerous young men dressed as Santas playing music, dancing, or selling knickknacks for young children. Christmas Day is marked by a series of social visits to family and friends in which hosts serve wine, liqueur, Arabic coffee, cookies or traditional sweets, and chocolate; young Christians may continue the celebration late into the evening with parties at restaurants and hotels.

It is not uncommon to find non-Christian Syrians who celebrate some aspect of Christmas, such as decorating a small fir tree indoors.

Easter

Easter is a major holiday for Syrian Christians, and if one spends any time in Christian areas in the week

beforehand, it's simply impossible to miss. Marking the end of the fasting and penance observed during Lent, it includes cross-bearing processions in the street replete with marching bands. Another public ritual associated with Easter is that of Holy Thursday, which in Arabic is called the "Thursday of Secrets" and falls on the last Thursday before Easter, on which occasion Damascene Christians visit seven different churches in the Old City, pausing in each one to pray. Syrian Christians celebrate Easter by attending special church services and with visits to their families and friends. Both the Catholic and Orthodox Easters (calculated according to the Gregorian and Julian calendars, respectively) are considered national holidays on which schools and government offices close.

'Ashura

Shi'ite Muslims celebrate 'Ashura during the first ten days of Muharram, the first month of the Islamic lunar year (so dates vary), in commemoration of the historical martyrdom of Hussein, son of Ali (the Prophet Muhammad's nephew and son-in-law), in a battle at Karbala in modern-day Iraq in 680 CE. Hussein was killed when he and his small band of followers fought against the much larger army of the Umayyad Caliph Yazid. In recognition of Hussein's martyrdom, and in penance for the failure of the rest of his followers to come to his aid, Shi'ite Muslims treat this period as one of intense mourning that culminates on the last day. They dress in black, decorate the streets with black banners, and attend gatherings at mosques and special halls called *husseiniyas* in which eulogies commemorating the martyrdom are recited. Outside shrines, food stands give out free tea, cookies, and other foods, to aid those who have made a pilgrimage to them in honor of the holiday—which is frequently the case at Syria's important Shi'ite shrines, which attract many pilgrims. Some men perform rituals of self-flagellation by cutting, beating, or striking themselves to express remorse that they were not able to stand with the Imam Hussein on that day— although certain religious leaders have condemned such practices, urging their followers to simply donate blood instead. In all cases, 'Ashura is a time of piety and communal spirit for Shi'ite Muslims.

Mawlids

A *mawlid*, a celebration of the birthday of the Prophet or another holy person, is generally a private, family-oriented affair, and unlike the major Islamic holidays mentioned above, is not necessarily celebrated by all Syrian Muslims. Neighborhoods that do observe the *mawlid* decorate their streets with green banners for the

occasion. A family holding a *mawlid* celebration
might invite relatives and close friends to their
home to participate in the singing of religious
songs, or to listen to a *Qur'an* recitation; they also
honor their guests by distributing small bags of
mulabbas, or sugarcoated almonds. Alternatively,
they might attend a similar celebration in a mosque.

Nowruz

While not really a religious holiday, Nowruz, the
celebration of the Kurdish New Year on the spring
equinox (usually March 21), is a major festival for
Syria's Kurdish population. In northeastern Syria,
where large numbers of Kurds are concentrated,
the festival is observed with somewhat raucous
celebrations in tents erected in fields in the
countryside, with dancing, eating, political speeches
about Kurdish rights, and enormous bonfires made
of wood and old tires. In town, Kurds line the
sidewalks with candles in paper lanterns. Women
in particular wear homemade traditional Kurdish

dresses, which are brightly colored and glittery, with a matching belt and scarf or headband for the hair, and a light, translucent overcoat. Nowruz's origins lie in a Zoroastrian holiday that's still celebrated in Iran, but for Syrian Kurds it means something quite different, as it's one of the few open expressions of a Kurdish identity that are permitted.

NATIONAL HOLIDAYS
New Year's Eve and Day
The New Year according to the Gregorian calendar (December 31–January 1) is celebrated throughout Syria with a mixture of small gatherings at home and large parties thrown by restaurants and hotels with live entertainment. Syrians typically call and text message their friends and family at midnight to wish them a happy new year, in numbers great enough to temporarily tie up the phone system.

Revolution Day
A commemoration (March 8) of the 1963 coup by which the Ba'ath Party first launched itself into the seat of power—one it continues to occupy to this day. The holiday is marked with patriotic television programs, but the average Syrian is unlikely to do anything special to observe it.

Teacher's Day
In honor of educators, teachers and university professors get the day (March 20) off, as do their students.

Mother's Day
On this day (March 21), Syrians honor their

mothers with gifts and other niceties such as a special dinner or a celebration with cake.

Independence Day
A commemoration of the day (April 17) in 1946 when the last French soldier left Syrian soil. Many celebrate this day with visits to a point from which it is possible to see the Israeli-occupied Golan Heights, as a reminder that not *all* foreign soldiers have left Syrian land. Otherwise, it is an occasion for picnicking, singing songs both patriotic and otherwise, and dancing.

Labor Day
Labor Day (May 1) is celebrated with patriotic television programming and organized, mandatory volunteer work for government employees, but the average Syrian just gets a day off.

Martyr's Day
This commemoration (May 6) of Syrian soldiers who've died at war is another holiday that most Syrians don't take a great interest in, but government officials may take part in activities such as a visit to the Tomb of the Unknown Soldier outside Damascus, and the president invites the children of "martyrs" to a special banquet.

Anniversary of the October War
A holiday (October 6) in remembrance of the beginning of the October War of 1973, in which Syria allied with Egypt against Israel. The war is seen as having restored Syrian pride after the devastating loss of 1967.

HOLIDAYS CELEBRATED IN SYRIA

RELIGIOUS HOLIDAYS	DATES
Ramadan and Eid al-Fitr (revelation of *Qur'an*)	Vary according to lunar calendar
Eid al-Adha (Abraham's sacrifice)	Varies according to lunar calendar
Christmas	December 25
Easter	Varies; falls on a Sunday in late March–early May
'Ashura (martyrdom of Hussein)	Varies according to lunar calendar
Nowruz (spring equinox)	Varies; often falls on March 20 or 21

NATIONAL HOLIDAYS	
New Year's Eve and Day	December 31–January 1
Revolution Day	March 8
Teacher's Day	March 20
Mother's Day	March 21
Independence Day	April 17
Labor Day	May 1
Martyr's Day	May 6
Anniversary of the October War	October 6

CHARMS AND FOLK BELIEFS

Religious practices are not the sole expression of spirituality and belief in Syria. This extends to folk beliefs that may have a religious cast or connection even though they are not officially enshrined in religious texts—such as the use of a *Qur'an* as a charm to ward off the "evil eye."

The Evil Eye

Many Syrians believe in the "evil eye," usually called just "the eye" or "the eye of envy" in Arabic, which implies a belief in the literally harmful power of a combination of a strong gaze, ill wishes, and covetous thoughts. For protection, Syrians often wear or carry charms that range from a miniature *Qur'an* to the image of a blue eye, and hang similar amulets on new cars or houses. As a kind of verbal charm, they use phrases such as *ma sha allah*, or "It's what God wishes," when praising people or belongings, as a sign of their good intentions and lack of a damaging gaze, or *khazayt al-'ayn*, when talking about someone with enviable good fortune or abilities. The arrival of a sudden misfortune may be traced back to the "evil eye," and an afflicted person can be treated in a number of ways, such as having a matriarch of their family place a hand on their head and reciting verses from the *Qur'an*.

Shrines

Although purist Sunni Islamists scorn worship at shrines as a harmful innovation in Islam, many Syrians visit shrines built around the tombs of holy Muslims from the past, such as the twelfth-century Sufi scholar Shaykh Muhi ad-Din ibn Arabi. The supplicants pray and recite from the *Qur'an* in the belief that the venerated figure can act as an intercessor between them and God. Many shrines are built into mosques, and some are quite flexible religiously, attracting both Muslims and Christians. The definition of *who* can be an intercessor seems equally flexible, as some Syrians perform similar devotionals at the grave of former President Hafez al-Asad—decidedly not a religious figure, but a powerful one nonetheless.

Shi'ite shrines, on the other hand, are a well established part of devotional practice, and Shi'ite Muslims from neighboring countries like Iraq and Iran make pilgrimages to the shrines of Sayyida Ruqayya (the daughter of the Imam Hussein) and Sayyida Zeinab (the daughter of the Imam Ali), located in and around Damascus. The atmosphere inside the beautiful Iranian-funded buildings that house these tombs often reaches a fever pitch, as the sight of the mausoleum is so moving for some that women weep and men faint, while others read from the *Qur'an*, pray with their heads resting on small cakes of dried soil from the battle site Karbala in modern-day Iraq, or wipe the tomb with cloths that they'll carry home with them as a keepsake that has imbibed some of the shrine's holy power.

Jinn

Jinn are malevolent spirits who may wreak havoc in the lives of mortals. They are mainly folkloric figures who don't play a large role in Syrian life, but since they're mentioned in the *Qur'an*, they're considered beings whose existence Muslims should believe in.

Fortune-telling
Coffee is an integral part of Syrian socializing, and since Arabic coffee is served with the grounds still in it, the dregs provide an excellent medium for reading the future—an activity that many Syrian women enjoy. After drinking their coffee, they turn their mugs upside down in the saucers so that the soupy mixture of grounds and coffee dries, then look for meaning in the designs now decorating the walls of the cups. These readings are all in good fun, but Syrians with difficulties in their personal life— such as a girl with no suitors—do sometimes turn to professional fortune-tellers for help, who may identify the celestial problem and prescribe a remedy. Such services are expensive, illegal, and disapproved of by the religious establishment.

chapter four

MAKING FRIENDS

Although observers sometimes stress the importance of family in Arab societies as a definitive point of difference with Western culture, Syrians also place a high value on close and long-lasting friendships. It's easier there, perhaps, to keep such relationships over years and decades: although families may move from the countryside to the city in search of work, they tend to stay rooted in the neighborhood they settle in and also retain close ties with their village of origin. Children growing up in a neighborhood and attending local schools keep many of the same friends through adulthood, and these remain an important factor in their lives even if they attend university and expand their social circle.

Having a friend is a significant time investment; there is no excuse for not joining one's friends several times a week to socialize for hours, and there are few barriers between really close friends: they may call each other at any time, speak to or see each other daily, borrow clothing, share meals, and are seen as being just as important as family. Some parts of Syrian society consider cross-gender friendships normal for young people and don't see time spent with friends of the opposite gender, particularly as part of a group, as a sign of romantic interest. In other, more conservative parts of society, cross-gender friendships are frowned upon, but same-gender friendships are as important as ever.

Friends are just as important to married Syrians as to young singles, of course, but the pressures of starting a family often decrease the amount of time available for them, and social life gradually takes on a more family-oriented nature. While gatherings among young people are informal and lack the ritualized hospitality of other Syrian visits, socializing takes on a more formal character when couples have established a home and family.

GETTING ALONG

Good manners are important in the Arab world. Saying "please," "thank you," and "excuse me" will get you far! A couple of more basic rules: greet people every time you see them, and say good-bye when they leave.

One of the most important aspects of good manners is sharing. A Syrian lighting a cigarette always offers one to their companions, even if they're nonsmokers. No food should be consumed in front of others without offering each of them a bite—and if you accept the bite, don't take any more than that unless the offer is repeated! No one who comes to the door of a home should leave without being invited in for a tea or coffee—you should decline the first offer, but accept if it is repeated.

Syrians are also experts in *mujaamala,* or flattery—in this context, it's a harmless sort that is simply part of good manners and understood by all. This includes things such as telling your acquaintances that you missed them, even if you didn't, and informing your guests that it's too early for them to leave, even if it's actually quite late. For merchants, it means saying things like "This shop is your shop!" to their customers, and pretending to refuse payment for goods and services. Don't be fooled—you are expected to insist on paying anyway! These are mere pleasantries that function as a form of social lubrication.

People are ready to help out with small favors, and don't want to appear to refuse help to someone—thus, they may offer directions to a place they don't really know the location of. On the other hand, those who are really able to help will do so, and if you're lost you may find that people want to walk you to your destination rather than just pointing the way.

ATTITUDES TOWARD FOREIGNERS
Friendship with Foreigners

The enthusiasm with which Syrians welcome foreigners to their country and even into their homes is one of the aspects of their society and culture that most surprises visitors. For Syrians, getting to know a foreigner can be a means of learning more about countries they're unlikely to see firsthand. They're often eager to get answers to persistent questions about life in the West, and to confirm or refute impressions shaped by American movies and TV shows. Talking with a foreigner can also be an opportunity to rescue, at least in part, Syria's blackened image in the Western media, or provide a chance to practice English. Sometimes Syrians who feel out of place in Syrian society seek out foreigners because they sense that they may be more open to certain ideas and viewpoints.

Foreigners who want to meet more Syrians need only display a friendly face and reach out to neighbors, coworkers, or classmates, while keeping an open mind. One American student in Damascus started chatting with a Syrian student on a microbus during her morning commute to class; the two girls ended up exchanging phone numbers and later became close friends and even shared a small apartment for a few months. Joining in clubs and other organized activities, like attending religious services, can be a good way to meet Syrians with similar interests. Students of Arabic can also get to know Syrians who are studying foreign languages by setting up a language exchange where each offers help or conversation practice in their native language.

While foreigners are by default granted some leniency in social rules, it is also important for them to follow some additional ones: listen to Syrians and their opinions of Syria before judging, and approach this complex country with humility. People love to ask foreigners their opinion of Syria; if you feel a need to mention a negative view of the country, temper it with praise. After all, the Syrians understand the downsides to their homeland better than any foreigner, and they want to know that you've seen the good side of it, as well.

Position of Foreign Women

As we have seen, it is not uncommon in certain parts of Syrian society for young men and women to have platonic friendships. Despite this fact, foreign women sometimes find it difficult to keep romantic interest from intruding into their friendships with Syrian men—and not just from the Syrian side. Misunderstandings, however, are particularly likely with men from conservative families for whom casual friendships with women are atypical; in this context, what foreign women see as ordinary friendliness is easily misread as flirtatious behavior. It's a cultural chasm that's reinforced by media stereotypes of Western women, whose behavior in Western films, movies, and TV shows is seen as promiscuous and undiscerning. That said, there is certainly no reason for foreign women to avoid being with friendly Syrian men, as there are also examples of successful and long-lasting friendships between the two.

Dating between Foreigners and Syrians
Dating between Syrian men and foreign women is quite common, while the opposite is rare. Syrian girls must always behave with an eye to their reputation, which can be damaged by spending too much time with men, even in public places. A girl's reputation would certainly be harmed if she were seen entering a man's home without supervision; a damaged reputation, in turn, would significantly decrease her chances of a good marriage. Moreover, many Western men lack the patience to proceed with a relationship as slowly as Syrian girls tend to be comfortable with. Exceptions exist, of course, but in general foreign men who want to date Syrian women should be aware that the honorable response to damaging a girl's reputation—particularly by engaging in premarital sex—is to marry her.

Syrian men, on the other hand, are often eager to date foreign women, sometimes because it frees them from the constraints that paying attention to a Syrian woman's reputation places upon them, or because marrying a Westerner is the ticket to a foreign residency card or passport that they would never be able to obtain otherwise. On the other hand, examples of relationships built on mutual love and respect also abound. Syrian men are often crushed, though, when their foreign girlfriend, who may have seen the relationship as only one in a long string of attachments that don't necessarily lead to any kind of long-term commitment, returns to her home country. Regardless of the circumstances, such relationships usually require an even greater effort at serious and clear communication than the average romantic encounter; and among those who have achieved this, there are also examples ending in satisfying long-term partnerships.

GREETINGS

If you run into a friend or acquaintance at an event or a restaurant, don't satisfy yourself with a casual wave: in Syria, greetings are an important mark of mutual esteem and courtesy that it would be extremely rude to forget. A proper greeting usually includes, at the very least, eye contact, a handshake, and a smile; many Syrians kiss each other lightly on each cheek while shaking hands, although more conservative men and women only kiss those of the same gender. Some men and women don't like to shake hands with the opposite sex, so it's appropriate for foreign men to wait for women to initiate a handshake, and vice versa; if they don't, it's appropriate to place your right hand over your heart instead.

It is also considered a mark of esteem to stand up to greet others. When someone enters a crowded room full of people they know, sometimes a simple wave and group greeting suffices; at other times, they might circulate, kissing and gripping the hands of a dozen or more acquaintances in succession. In familial or formal settings, it's polite to greet the most important person in the room first—usually the oldest male. The most conservative decorum demands that men be greeted before women, but it is also acceptable to greet the oldest male first and then everyone else in the order in which they are standing or sitting near to him.

Greetings in Arabic rely on a simple principle: whatever someone wishes upon you, you must return it back to them, preferably with *more* of the same—which means that you cannot simply mirror the greeting you have received. If a friend wishes you the usual *sabah al-kheir*, "a morning of goodness," then you should reply with hopes for, at the very least, *sabah an-nur*, "a morning of light." The formal greeting of *as-salaamu aleikum*, "peace be upon you," should be countered with *wa aleikum as-salaam*: "and upon you peace," while the casual greeting of *marhaba*, a simple hello, necessitates a reply of *marhabtain*, or two hellos. This principle can even be applied to foreign words: one may hear upper-class Syrians greeting each other with *bonjour* and replying with two *bonjours*: *bonjourein*!

The basics of greetings don't stop there, however. It is important to follow greetings with a series of inquiries: *keefak*? "how are you?" and *shu akhbarak*? "what's your news?" are necessities; if time and interest allows, it is also good manners to inquire about health and family members.

The way in which one bids friends good-bye is also important, as it should mirror how they were greeted. Whether kisses, a handshake, or a hand over the heart was appropriate for the greeting, that's what should be repeated upon leaving. When Syrians bid friends farewell, they often ask, *biddek shi?*, that is, "Do you want or need anything (from me)?" Some foreigners, confused, reply with a simple "no," but the proper response is *salamtek*: "(I want) your health and well-being."

With people you see very often—daily, for example—it's not necessary to go to all the lengths described here; these are the circumstances in which a casual wave and hello/good-bye is certainly appropriate.

HOSPITALITY
Invitations Out

A typical meal out is large, so bring your appetite! Inviting foreigners out to eat is a way of welcoming them and demonstrating Syrian hospitality, notably among those who have the money to pay for a meal in a restaurant, something that's much more expensive than cooking at home. A restaurant meal usually consists of a course of appetizers, or *mezze*, then main dishes—often various roasted meats, or *kebabs*—fruit for dessert, and finally tea or coffee, served as a feast that often lasts up to three hours (you should stay for the whole thing). At the end, one person may pay for the meal, if they are hosting the gathering, or the diners split the check equally among themselves. It would be rude to haggle over what particular people ate or ordered. If the meal includes more than one family, the family heads often make a show of arguing over who will have the honor of footing the bill, although the one who extended the invitation in the first place should win. It is polite to reciprocate the invitation later, if one is able.

When groups of young people who have similar, limited incomes dine out together, no one is expected to pay the whole bill themselves or even to offer; rather, it is common to split it.

Invitations Home

Syrians take pride in their hospitality and are eager to demonstrate it for guests, so it is not uncommon for a casual conversation with a Syrian to turn into a coffee or lunch invitation. It's all right to decline politely at first, and then, if it is repeated, to accept the offer as genuine. If one is truly unable to accept an invitation, it is important to express the heartfelt hope that you can take it up in the future.

Invitations for lunch, the most important meal of the day, are most common, but don't show up at noon—or anywhere close! Lunch usually begins

between 2:00 and 4:00 p.m., but it's a good idea to ask your host when they'd like you to come—something that's also true if they invite you over in the evening. Expect to spend around three hours at someone's home for such an occasion, which will probably include socializing beforehand, a salad along with other

appetizers, a main dish, then fruit and tea or coffee afterward, along with more relaxing and socializing. It would be impolite to rush through these steps in the hope of leaving early, so be sure to allow enough time! Even an invitation to drink coffee at home will usually involve some presentation of fresh fruit or small cookies. You'll typically share such a meal with the entire family, if they're home.

Best Behavior
It is good manners to bring some sort of gift to the home of someone who has invited you over for a meal, but unless you are absolutely certain that your hosts drink alcohol and were planning on having it with the meal, it is best not to bring wine or spirits (remember, observant Muslims do not drink alcohol). A nice box of candies is a typical, very acceptable gift.

It also important to show appreciation for the food, which a Syrian housewife (or working wife who doubles as housewife in her spare time) has spent hours preparing and takes great pride in presenting, both by complimenting her on the food and by eating as much of it as you are comfortably able. Try to eat at least one serving of each dish. Your hosts may seem to want to fill you to the bursting point, often putting more onto your plate than you can manage, but after they've served you one plateful, you can politely avoid overloading by insisting on serving yourself, then doing so slowly and in moderate portions.

Some households, when faced with a large number of guests, serve food not on the table but on a spread of newspapers on the floor, onto which it is appropriate to toss leftover bones or seeds, etc., as the newspapers will simply be gathered up and thrown out afterward.

A phrase commonly heard during any meal is *sahtain*, or "health twice over," to which it is polite to reply, *'ala albek*, that is, "upon your heart!" When you're full and don't want to eat any more, you may easily signal it by saying *al-hamdu lillah*, ("thank God"), or *daimeh*, to which your companion should reply *bi-wujuudak* (the two phrases indicate that you both hope to always eat this sort of good food together).

EATING ETIQUETTE

Watch what the Syrians do, and eat as they do:

- The food is served and eaten communally, and diners are provided with small individual plates onto which they transfer small helpings of every dish, though some prefer to eat directly out of the shared bowls.
- Although knives and forks are usually provided (at least in restaurants), many foods are eaten with the help of the flat bread that's provided with every meal: diners tear off small pieces and use them to scoop up the food.
- If you are dining from a communal plate, it's polite to scoop only from the side nearest to you.
- When eating, always use your right hand (never your left).

You should stay for all the courses and be prepared to drink coffee or tea after a meal, rather than rushing out. Pave the way for your exit by suggesting that you must leave in a little while, rather than right away, in order to allow for some back-and-forth as the hosts insist that their guest stays longer. Once you've drunk tea or coffee (slowly!) and socialized a little, it is acceptable to take requests that you stay a while longer still less seriously, and to actually leave.

TIME
For Syrians, friendship is a significant time investment—sometimes much more than foreigners realize. The idea of maintaining a friendship by meeting to drink coffee for an hour or so every week would be strange: social engagements normally last several hours and occur frequently. On weekends, an all-day outing lasting twelve hours or more is par for the course. For foreigners in Syria who already feel busy with their studies or work, such differences in the perception of time can cause friction in their friendships with Syrians. For other foreigners, the value that Syrians place on spending time with friends rather than reaping material rewards from work is one of the many things that make life in Syria enjoyable.

MAKING CONVERSATION
The universal rules of polite conversation apply in Syria as they would anywhere else: don't bring up sex, religion, or (domestic) politics with anyone you don't know well. There are, however, countless appropriate conversational topics; here are just a few suggestions. At the most superficial level, it's

always safe to make small talk about the beauty of Syria, which tourist sites you've visited or plan to visit, or Syrian food. It's also good to ask someone about their children and tell them about yours.

Although it isn't impolite to talk about school and work, Syrians are generally less enthusiastic than Americans, in particular, about going into these subjects in great depth. Asking about favorite movies, television shows, and singers can be a great way to find out more about Syrian culture and possibly discover points of common interest. Syrians tend to be soccer enthusiasts, so bring it up if you are too. Asking about a family's history and place of origin in Syria can also encourage some interesting memories.

It's fine to discuss international politics or your country's political system, but if you support Israel, don't say so, and don't criticize the Syrian president or his father. If you're an atheist, you'll be more comfortable if you don't announce that, either. But in close friendships, as everywhere, many of these barriers can fall.

HUMOR

Syrians appreciate a good joke, and their humor tends to be situational and satirical. One of the most popular television shows to come out every year during Ramadan is *Buqa'at ad-Daw* (*The Spotlight*), which consists of short skits poking fun at all manner of social situations.

Another television mini-mini-series (each episode was only a few minutes long) called *There's No Hope* satirized the Syrian love of television by presenting a character who was so poor that he lived in a one-room house with his wife and children, and yet still paid for satellite service. When he considered canceling the service because he didn't want his children to see violence on the evening news, his hapless companion told him not to be silly; rather than cancel, he should turn to a channel that wasn't broadcasting anything instead!

Other favorite targets of Syrian humor include the inefficiency and bureaucracy of their own government, as well as their fellow countrymen— especially the residents of Homs, a city a few hours north of Damascus who are the butt of many Syrian wisecracks.

The Wise Men of Homs

There was a big hole in the ground near the entrance to Homs, and people were always falling in and then having to be taken to the hospital. After a time, the city's three wisest men held a meeting in order to discuss and solve the problem. The first said: Let's dig all of Homs downward so that it's level with the bottom of the hole. The second said: No, let's build a hospital next to the hole to treat those who fall in it. The third said: No, let's fill in this hole and dig another one next to the current hospital.

Jokes like this target the inefficiency of the country's leadership (and the perpetual nature of any construction project, which always begins with digging a large pit!), in addition to the hapless residents of Homs.

chapter five

PRIVATE & FAMILY LIFE

THE HOUSEHOLD

The family is the centerpiece of Syrian life and plays a large role in everything from socializing to major life decisions. Syrians value their families and spend quite a lot of time with them—aunts, uncles, cousins, and all the like included. Families are, however, gradually shrinking: while Syrians who are now passing middle age might regale you with tales of eight, ten, or even more siblings, the current average is just over three children per woman.

Islam does permit men to marry up to four women, but such arrangements are also increasingly rare—not to mention unheard of among Syria's Christians and Muslim minority sects, which never sanctioned such arrangements in the first place. Islam demands that those with more than one wife treat all of them equally, and most men don't have the material resources to do so; nor do their wives usually welcome the idea. Hence, households are increasingly nuclear. Divorce certainly occurs, but remains relatively uncommon—not surprising in light of the fact that marriage is seen not merely as an expression of romantic love but as a social and economic arrangement, optimized not only for the man and woman involved but also for their extended families and for the children they bear.

Men are considered to be the head of the household, and are responsible for providing materially for their dependents. The tightening economic straitjacket does mean that women work outside the home more frequently than in the past— something that some women welcome as a chance to develop new skills and talents, and others scorn as a burden and a distraction from the child rearing they'd rather focus on. Indeed, even when women are employed outside, they typically continue to bear the primary responsibility for housework, cooking, and child care.

In a country where economic opportunities are few, the state is slow to change, and civil society is restricted, family steps in to fill the gaps. Relatives provide child care, help arrange job opportunities, and care for those who cannot look after themselves. Homes for the elderly are rare, and putting one's parents into such an assisted living arrangement would be regarded as a gross departure from filial duty. As in other matters, personal happiness and convenience is secondary in comparison to the importance of family. Even when they live separately, children usually remain in close contact with their parents and siblings, and the family often reserves one day a week to gather together if they live close enough to do so.

LIVING SPACE

The traditional urban home still survives in the oldest parts of Syria's major cities, where most of the houses are built in the "Arab" style: rooms arranged in a rectangle open inward onto a roofless courtyard adorned with a fountain, fruit tree, or other greenery, while a fenced balcony runs around the inside of the upper stories, connecting the rooms. The smallest of these houses have several bedrooms, while the largest might have more than a dozen—an incredible sight that can be witnessed at some of the restaurants that have been opened in restored houses.

This type of home was once common in less ancient parts of Syrian cities as well, but population pressures and changing family structures have resulted in their replacement with apartment buildings. Traditionally, a Damascene house provided space for several generations of the same family: when male children grew up and married, they would bring their wives to live with them in the house where they had grown up with their parents, then raise their own children in the same space. Women went to live with their husbands' families in a similar arrangement. In such a household, the oldest male was the patriarch, and his wife usually exerted considerable influence over the household, including her children's wives and their children.

More recently, however, the nuclear rather than extended family has become the favored basic family unit. Many of the Arab-style houses outside the Old City of Damascus, for instance, were either partitioned to give each family more autonomy, or demolished to make way for apartment buildings, in which the same male descendants who would have once lived together could each occupy a different apartment with their wife and children, remaining close to the extended family but with greater physical separation. Housewives also tend to prefer apartments to traditional houses, which require

much more attention to keep clean. As prices rose in some areas and families grew, these extended clans were increasingly scattered across cities, although they tended to retain close ties nonetheless.

DAILY LIFE

Daily life differs greatly among Syrians, depending on whether they're urban or rural, wealthy, middle class, or poor, but very broadly speaking they tend to go to work or school in the morning and, midafternoon, come home to eat lunch around 3:00 p.m. with their families, then either return to work or spend the rest of the day with their families and friends, often watching TV or drinking coffee and tea with neighbors. The weekend in Syria—like much of the Middle East—is on Friday and Saturday, and Friday is usually reserved for an outing of some sort with relatives or friends, preferably a picnic in an area of natural beauty if weather permits, while Saturday is a chance to rest, work, or catch up on errands.

Shopping

Shopping for necessities usually takes place at the small shops that fill every neighborhood, too small individually to accommodate more than two or three customers, and very specialized: one shop might sell mainly dairy products such as yogurt, milk, and cheese, another fruits and vegetables, and a third basic packaged foods. Since there's a high degree of integration between residential and commercial areas in cities and towns, most daily shopping needs can be met within several blocks of one's home. Similarly, clothing purchases generally take place at smaller stores or citywide chains that reflect a local sense of style, while wealthier Syrians may shop at the Western brand-name stores that have opened branches in the country in the last few years. A few Western-style malls have recently opened on the outskirts of the larger cities, where one can purchase all sorts of products not generally available in the city, but their high prices make them an unlikely destination for the average Syrian shopper.

Syrian women usually take great pride in their cooking skills. They prefer to cook mostly from

scratch, using fresh ingredients, and look down on the idea of buying preprepared items and packaged meals. One market in Damascus that famously offers plastic-wrapped, prechopped vegetables is known as *suq at-tanaabal,* or "the lazy person's market"!

GROWING UP IN SYRIA
Children

Children are highly valued in Syrian culture. Having children is one of the major goals of marriage, and raising them one of a wife's most important duties—to such an extent that some of those who argue for the improvement of women's education do so on the grounds that it will enable them to be better mothers! The approach to child care, however, tends to be more relaxed than it is in the West. Syrian women prefer to rely on their own instincts and the advice of older friends and relatives rather than devour child care manuals before

giving birth. Children are regarded as resilient and may perform small errands for their parents and play with their peers in the street from a young age. In close-knit communities, the temporary disappearance of a child isn't a cause for alarm because it will inevitably be watched over by nearby friends and relatives, and the dark specters that haunt the American parent's imagination—kidnapping, child molestation, and the like—seem equally far off.

Youth Culture

The youth of Syria are both forward-looking and frustrated. They are better educated than their parents, excited to embrace what the future might offer—privatization and commensurate economic opportunities, the possibilities presented by telecommunications, travel, and study abroad—and stymied in their attempts to do so by the pressures of life, by an economy that's not growing fast enough to absorb them, by a poor Internet infrastructure, by an inflexible education system, by the difficulty of obtaining visas to visit and study in other countries, and by networks of patronage that make *whom* you know more useful in getting ahead than *what* you know.

Economic Pressures and "Waithood"

Young people generally live at home until they marry, unless they travel to a different city in order to work or study. But getting married isn't always easy: home ownership—in which the ownership of apartments is included—is considered one of the most important hallmarks of security and stability, so many families would be reluctant to permit their daughter to marry a man who did not yet own an apartment. This is a source of considerable anxiety for young men for whom such a goal is increasingly difficult to attain before their late twenties or early thirties, due to a brutal combination of rising property prices and stagnant salaries. A 2008 bank advertisement for home loans played on such fears. The ad asked Syrians, "Why the wait?" and depicted an elderly man in a suit tenderly holding a gray-haired woman in a white dress on his arm. In another variation on the same theme, a poverty-stricken character on Syrian TV was able to marry the equally penurious girl of his dreams only by selling one of his kidneys in order to buy a house.

Such a drastic measure isn't realistic, of course, but the desperation the scenario expresses can be very real. The importance of having a good job, salary, and home secured before one's wedding makes taking the step to marriage—the only way most young Syrians move out of their family homes and into adulthood—a difficult one to take. Although young women aren't expected to earn enough money to buy a home, they tend to have less freedom as young adults than their male counterparts, and the pressure to find an adequate husband can also be intense. Some have termed this period of life for Middle Eastern youth "waithood," and they're not wrong—although in Syria, stuck as they may be, young people do far more than sit around while they wait. They work, even if not in jobs that match their skill level; they spend time with family; they go out with friends; they attend cultural events, if they have the time and money; and they look for better opportunities.

Education

Syria's educational system can boast some major achievements, having drastically increased the country's literacy rate to 80 percent over the past few decades, a number that's even higher among the younger generation. School attendance is mandatory through the ninth grade, and free through university. Syrian curricula do, however, rely heavily on lectures and rote memorization, with less emphasis on independent study work and critical thinking.

Public primary schools are generally mixed-gender, while public secondary schools are gender-segregated; private schools might be either. In ninth grade, students take a national exam whose results determine whether they go on to high school or to special vocational schools. In high school, students choose to concentrate on either sciences or humanities, a choice that limits the subjects they can study in college. Even more important in this regard is the *thanawiya a'ama*, the final, nationwide comprehensive high school exam that crowns the high school experience of all graduating seniors. Each student's score on this difficult test determines in which departments he or she may study at university, with the highest score cutoffs reserved for medicine, dentistry, pharmacy, and other scientific pursuits. Students study within a single discipline from the beginning of their time at university until the end, and there is very little flexibility in their choice of classes.

Syrian public universities are often overcrowded and uninspiring, sometimes with more students assigned to each lecture than can physically fit into the room; in any case, many students don't attend their lectures at all, but rather are in paid employment during the week and take time off at the end of each semester to take their exams. On the upside, however, these public universities are free for those with qualifying *thanawiya a'ama* scores, meaning that while the playing field between rich and poor isn't exactly level, at least they both have a more equal chance of completing a degree once they've gained admission.

In the past few years, a number of private universities have been established in Syria, some on an openly for-profit basis. For those who can pay (the tuition is usually far more than the average Syrian makes in a year), they offer a flexible admissions policy that allows students to follow their interests and not just their high school results, studying subjects for which their *thanawiya a'ama* scores would have disqualified them at a public university. They also boast smaller classes, a more discussion-based teaching style, and the chance to brush up on one's English as this is the language in which many courses are taught. Some criticize these universities, however, as a way for the elite to funnel their children through college and into family-reserved company jobs. The growth of the private education sector can only serve to exacerbate the gap between Syria's haves and have-nots.

Military Service

The military has long been a vehicle for social mobility in Syria—former President Hafez al-Asad, for instance, used it to move out of a poor mountain village, through the ranks of the Air Force, and eventually into the country's highest office—and it remains so for the country's poorer and rural youth, who find escape and opportunities in the compulsory twenty-one-month military service that all men over eighteen (except for only sons) must perform; Palestinian refugees also serve, even though they're not Syrian citizens. The military service policy, however, dogs the country's middle-class urban youth, who generally see little reason to spend nearly two years of their lives serving in miserable and demoralizing conditions, doing work that utilizes few of their skills, for only a few dollars per month in compensation.

When men inside Syria are called up for service, the government doesn't actively come and snatch them from their homes if they fail to report—instead, it puts their names on a list at all border crossings, airports, and police stations, so that they'll be picked up if they try to leave the country or commit a crime. Men can put off military service as long as they're enrolled in some institute of higher education, and those with the means can pay the official fee, equivalent to US $5,000, to get out of service—as long as they've spent at least five years outside the country. (Depending on one's circumstances, even more complicated rules and exceptions can apply.) Thus, educated young men who might otherwise try to put their talents to use inside Syria receive an extra push to seek work abroad, and even those who remain in the country expend considerable energy trying to dodge the draft.

Work Abroad
A number of factors, including military service and low wages, push Syrian men to seek work abroad. Women also travel abroad for work, sometimes to accompany a husband or other family member, but traditionally minded families are less likely to accept the idea of a woman studying or working abroad on her own. Syria's poor international image, as well as the current Western mistrust of immigrants in general and Muslims in particular, mean that it's difficult for Syrians to obtain visas for work or study in the Europe or the United States. It's much easier to obtain work visas in the oil-rich Gulf countries, constantly in need of manpower to fuel their booming economies and offering salaries that to Syrians seem astronomical by comparison.

Dating and Engagement
The range of dating and marriage practices within Syria is wide, varying not only according to the

religion, class, and geographical location, but by personal and familial preference as well. One of the most traditional ideals is that of marriage between paternal first cousins, and some Syrian spouses still refer to each other affectionately as "cousin," even if they're not related by blood. In the case of marriage between nonrelatives, conservative families prefer the suitor (with his father or another senior male relative) to approach the parents of his chosen bride and ask their permission to become affianced before even speaking to the girl, whom he might have spotted on the street and inquired about, or heard about from a female relative who'd searched for a marriageable girl on his behalf.

In this model, the engagement is a chance for the couple to get to know one another and to break it off if things don't go well. There are other young Syrians, however, who date before getting engaged, something that typically consists of talking on the phone and outings to restaurants and cafés. Such relationships follow a variety of rules—for instance, men usually initiate them and take responsibility for paying for the meals, cultural events, and the like.

Choosing a spouse generally remains a collaborative affair between parents and their children, varying from parents who vet potential partners before suggesting them to their children, to those who merely give consent to their children's choices. In any case, a successful marriage is thought to require the express agreement of all the parties involved—not parents who force their choices upon their children, or children who select a spouse without regard for their parents' input—because marriage is a joining of two families and not just two individuals.

What's permissible in terms of dating differs between families, but the rules are always much stricter for women than for men. Some families don't want their daughters to spend any time with nonrelated men, while others are fine with cross-gender friendships but not dating, and some are willing to permit chaste premarriage dating. Women's virginity at the time of marriage remains of paramount importance for the vast majority of Syrian families, since even men who have no problem going out with nonvirgins usually don't want to marry them. But if anything's certain in Syrian dating, it's that Syrian youth like to push the envelope beyond what's officially allowed, and a good deal more is going on behind the scenes than is immediately obvious.

FAMILY OCCASIONS
Birth
Birth is a joyous occasion, and one that involves a great deal of care and attention for the new mother and her child. Syrian women may give birth at home or in the hospital, but tend to remain in their houses for forty days after the birth, during which time they receive relatives, friends, and neighbors as well-wishers who come bearing gifts of money, clothing, amulets, and other baby accessories. Visitors may praise the beauty of the newborn, but not without invoking the name of God—saying *ma sha allah* ("it's what God willed") to signal their good intentions and ward off the "evil eye."

Birth control is not prohibited by Islam unless its goal is to prevent the birth of children entirely; using it to space out one's children, on the other hand, is permissible, and this is the use to which many Muslim Syrian women put it. Abortion is illegal but not difficult to obtain, and though frowned upon it does not provoke the same exaggerated passions attached to it in countries like the United States.

Weddings

Marriage is an exciting occasion and a serious milestone in life, one that signals a real move to adulthood. However the bride and groom may have met, the path toward marriage begins with an engagement, which may be celebrated with a small party and an exchange of rings, to be worn on the index finger of the right hand.

The range of wedding practices in Syria, like everything else, is quite varied. Some families hold gender-segregated weddings, others mixed, but they usually take place in the evening in a large rented hall with tables and a dance floor for both modern "Eastern" style dancing—also known as belly dancing—and the traditional *debke* (a circular folk dance). Guests typically arrive first to dance and socialize before the bride makes her appearance. If the wedding is gender-segregated, the bride usually enters the women's celebration alone to dance with her guests, who will have dressed in bright, revealing, and extravagant dresses. The groom enters a little while later, but not before a flurry of commotion overtakes the chamber as the women who were wearing low-cut dresses and elaborate hairstyles cover themselves in robes, long jackets, and head scarves. When the groom is present, the newlyweds

switch their rings from their right to left index
fingers, in order to publicly symbolize their bond,
before dancing together alone. While the wedding
may or may not include dinner, it will mostly
certainly include cake—usually a large white one,
sometimes cut for the first time by the bride and
groom gripping a decorated sword. Dancing may
continue into the early hours of the next morning.

If you're invited to a wedding in Syria, dress
smartly in order to show your respect for the couple,
but it's not necessary to bring a gift. If you are
female and invited to a gender-segregated wedding,
don't attempt to take pictures! Women tend to dress
in revealing outfits for these single-gender events,
and would be disturbed by the thought that a
nonrelated male might view your photograph. At
a mixed-gender wedding or the all-male part of
a segregated one, photographs should be fine.

For Muslims, the legal side of marriage—signing
the marriage contract and registering it in court—
requires only the witnesses to be present, so while
marriage is integral to the fulfillment of one's
religious and social duties, it doesn't call for a public
religious ceremony. Some marriages, however, are
performed *only* in front of a religious figure, often
clandestinely, and these, known as *zawaaj 'urfi*
(customary marriage), are not legally binding unless
they're registered officially in court. Marriage is a
social, legal, and material contract—not a sacrament.

Funerals

Rituals and customs can be an anchor in times of
extreme grief, and Syrian funerary practices are no
exception, determining the precise details of how
to mourn—again, with great variation between

religious groups, sects, and even villages. Islam requires that the body be ritually washed and buried as soon after death as possible, and it is usually the male family members who carry the coffin through the streets to the graveyard, where it is interred with the reading of Qur'anic verses. The next day, a special prayer for the soul of the departed is offered at noon.

Over the next three days the immediate family holds a gathering in the deceased's memory— sometimes in their home, sometimes in a tent erected in a public space, sometimes with separate hours for male and female vistors. Friends and relatives come to offer their condolences, drink bitter coffee, and read a Qur'anic verse for the soul of the departed. The family may also hire someone to recite from the *Qur'an* or play a recorded version. After the initial three-day mourning period, the family holds a similar gathering on each Thursday of the next forty days, and then every year on the anniversary of the death. Many also honor the occasion by distributing food or money to the poor.

If you are invited to a funeral or memorial gathering, dress simply and wear black. Unnecessary decorative touches, such as makeup or showy jewelry, are inappropriate. Do not send flowers— this would be particularly insensitive as these would imply happiness. There are many suitable phrases in Arabic that one can say to a bereaved person, but "I'm sorry" isn't one of them, as it sounds awkwardly as if the speaker were taking personal responsibility for the death. Instead, traditional expressions such as "*al-hayaat illak*," "Life is yours," or "*allah yarhamu*," "May God have mercy on him," convey condolences much more appropriately.

TIME OUT

Syrians place a high value on their leisure time,
despite the rising cost of living that forces many
to work long hours at more than one job in order
to make ends meet. Off the job—in the late
afternoons, evenings, and weekends, depending
on their work schedule—they spend their time
eating at home and at restaurants, drinking coffee,
and smoking *argileh* (a hookah, or water pipe),
watching television, shopping, picnicking, and
generally relaxing with family or friends. Syrians
like to socialize in groups, and the more who join
them the merrier. Even individual activities are
socially oriented: a Syrian who wants to read the
newspaper after work will probably sit with his or
her family to do so rather than in a private place.

Spending excessive amounts of time in solitary pursuits is not well regarded; free time is expected to be passed with the important people in one's life.

SYRIAN CUISINE

Eating out is a popular pastime for the urban young and for families, and many restaurants are filled with diners until well past midnight. The simplest food stands serve only a few dishes to be eaten at small plastic tables, while the most opulent dining establishments offer a feast for the senses: visual beauty, good food, and even *oud* (Arabic lute) players and singers at night for added entertainment. The vast majority of restaurants serve Syrian-style cooking and reliably include most of the same dishes, while the few foreign-food venues are  generally less popular and of uncertain quality.

Syria's cuisine has much in common with that of Lebanon, Jordan, and Palestine, but there are some local variations on certain dishes: in Syria, fava beans (known as *fuul*) are eaten whole with olive oil or a thin yogurt rather than mashed into a paste as in neighboring countries, for example, and Aleppian cuisine is known for its spiciness.

Despite variations in the quality and methods of preparation, there is a surprising uniformity to the dishes on offer in Syrian restaurants, which does not reflect the great range and diversity of home-cooked Syrian food. The dishes mentioned here are some of the most commonly available in restaurants, but the list is by no means exhaustive.

Appetizers

The meal usually begins with several of the small appetizers called *mezze* or *muqabilaat*, eaten communally. Some of the most common are

hummous and *musabbaha* (both are essentially a chickpea paste; the latter has extra toppings), *baba ghanouj* and *mutabbal* (eggplant paste mixed with chopped vegetables), *muhammara* (a spicy mix of ground walnuts and peppers), *batata miqliya* (French fries), *yalanji* (cooked rice wrapped in vine leaves, similar to the Greek dolmades), *kibbe* (ground lamb) served *niyye* (raw), *miqliyye* (fried in dough), or *mishwiyye* (grilled in dough), *shurbat a'ds* (smooth lentil soup), *tabouleh* (parsley salad), and *fattoush* (a delicious vegetable salad topped with chips of fried or toasted bread).

Main Dishes

Syrian restaurants tend not to serve individualized main dishes; diners are meant to order several and share them among a group. By far the most prevalent are *kebab* (ground meat packed around skewers and grilled), *kebab halabi* ("Aleppian kebab," a spicier version of the same dish), *shish tawuuq* (grilled chicken on skewers), and *furuuj mishwi* (a whole grilled chicken). Vegetarianism is uncommon in Syria, which is reflected in the selection of main dishes, so vegetarians will be better off filling themselves with appetizers.

Rare Treats
It would be impossible to do justice here to the great variety of foods that Syrians cook at home. Three dishes that are often eaten at home and occasionally served in restaurants are *maqlubeh* (rice cooked with spices and eggplant), *mulukhiyye* (stewed green leaves of the Jew's Mallow plant, usually served with rice), and *kusa mahshi* (zucchini stuffed with a mixture of rice and ground meat, then cooked in tomato sauce).

Fruits and Vegetables
Fresh fruits and vegetables are available everywhere in Syria and are quite cheap. If you visit in the spring, summer, or early fall, take the opportunity to make a snack of the delicious fresh fruit available at street-side stands (just wash it before eating). Produce is generally grown locally and is only available in season.

TIPS ON TIPPING

Tipping is an integral part of Syrian life: it can be a way of redistributing wealth and increasing the salaries of those who make very little, or a method of ensuring the favor of those whose services one uses often (sometimes this practice can shade into bribery). As a rule, anyone who performs a service as part of their job probably expects a tip. It should only be withheld in cases of extraordinarily bad service or rude behavior (remember that Syrian salaries are low and that this is a way of compensating). Someone who gives you directions, information, or help out of sheer friendliness does not expect a tip, and would be offended if you offered it.

Some guidelines:
Restaurants: 5–10 percent of the bill.
Hookah: 25–50 SP. Tip the hookah-tender (the one who brings you the hookah and changes your coals) separately from the waiter.
Taxi: 5–25 SP depending on the length of your journey. But bear in mind that paying a little more than the metered price is not considered so much a tip as a requisite charge to compensate for the rising cost of living.
Bathroom attendant: 10–25 SP.
Bellhop or other suitcase-carrier: 50 SP per suitcase.
Guides and hired drivers: 10–15 percent of their fee.

REFUELING FAST

Syrian fast food makes a quick and delicious snack, whether you're in between meals or looking for a low-cost substitute for one. Sold out of simple kiosks on the street or mini-restaurants with three or four tables, Syria's fast food offerings include:

saj a sandwich made of thin dough cooked over a heated iron dome and with spreads like *zaatar* (thyme and olive oil), *muhammara*, (spicy ground walnuts and peppers), or cheese

shawarma a tube-shaped sandwich made of chicken or another meat cooked on an enormous conical skewer, rolled up in flat bread with mayonnaise and pickles

falafel deep-fried balls of seasoned ground chickpeas, served by itself or as part of a sandwich

fuul whole fava beans served with olive oil (*zeit*) or a thin yogurt (*lebn*)

fatta strips of bread cooked in tahina and ghee and sometimes topped with meat or chicken

CAFÉ CULTURE

Coffeehouses have a long history in the Middle East. The first in Damascus was established in 1530, and they became omnipresent in the 1800s, functioning as a public space for men to exchange news, debate politics, and relax. Whiling away the hours in a smoky café, ordering one drink after another over games of cards or backgammon and a hookah, is still a popular way for Syrian men to spend their free time. Such establishments typically serve tea, coffee, *zuhuuraat* (herbal tea), and hookahs, but not food. Many men are regulars at their neighborhood cafés and know most of the other patrons, but these establishments remain distinctly male-dominated spaces that women rarely frequent alone, although they may go to some as part of mixed groups.

Western-style coffee shops, often part of foreign chains, are also becoming increasingly common, serving drip coffee and espresso along with wireless Internet for prices that exceed the daily income of some Syrians. Naturally they're mostly frequented by the young and wealthy, and seeing women visit them alone is usual and common.

DRINKS: TEA, COFFEE, JUICE, AND ALCOHOL

Beverages, whether alcoholic or not, are an important lubricant of Syrian social life; tea or coffee is the least that will be served at any home visit or outing. Since it is inconceivable that anyone would want to sit and relax without enjoying a hot drink, some enterprising individuals have made a business serving tea and coffee out of large thermos flasks in parks, wandering among the public relaxing in the greenery to take their orders and returning with a drink in exchange for 25–50 SP. This arrangement combines the convenience of a café with the pleasure of sitting in the open air.

The tea most often served in Syria is Lipton brand black tea (known as "red tea" in Arabic), although you can also ask for green tea (*shay akhdar*) or herbal tea *(zuhuuraat)*. Coffee is either Nescafé or the famously strong Arabic coffee that is made by boiling coffee grounds and water in a special coffeepot. Sugar is added while the coffee is being made, not afterward, so specify how sweet you like your coffee when you order: *sada* (no sugar), *khafif* (light sugar), *wasat* (medium), or *helu* (heavy sugar). Fresh juice is also available from juice stands, according to what's in season; order it in a clear glass mug to drink it there, or in a wax paper cup to take with you.

While the majority of Syrians do not drink alcohol, a significant minority does. Muslims are prohibited by their faith, but this is not legally enforced and is left instead to personal choice and social pressure. Even nondrinkers may be tolerant of those who choose to drink alcohol in their homes or in restaurants, but it is polite not to be ostentatious or to talk excessively about alcohol with those who choose not to partake. A common local alcoholic drink is *araq,* a kind of aniseed liquor, which is drunk mixed with water and ice; beer, wine, and spirits are also drunk and can be purchased at liquor

stores. Many restaurants and bars offer only Syrian and Lebanese wine, in which case it's a much safer bet to go with the Lebanese option (just ask for Ksara, the name of the winemaker). Commercially produced Syrian wine has very little to recommend it and should be consumed only in circumstances of financial duress.

SHOPPING AND BARGAINING

Bargaining is integral to the Syrian marketplace, so don't expect to pay the first price quoted to you, even if the item carries a written price tag. Bargaining isn't always appropriate, of course: it would be odd to haggle seriously over necessities such as fruits, vegetables, or bread, and the local branches of Western chain stores also operate on fixed prices. When shopping for souvenirs, clothing from local shops, and other medium-priced products, it's perfectly fine, and expected, to ask for a discount on the marked price; the same goes for larger expenditures, such as the monthly rent of an apartment.

BARGAINING FOR FUN AND PROFIT

• Don't show too much interest in the object you have half an eye on.

• Ask the shopkeeper how much he wants for a particular item before offering a price yourself. Then complain a bit about how expensive it is (in a friendly way!) and ask if he'll reconsider. This will give you an idea of how flexible he'll be.

• If you counter by offering a new price, start much lower than you *actually* think is fair, since your goal is to meet the shopkeeper in the middle.

• If the first price you offer is immediately accepted, your offer is too high!

• Aim for a 25 percent discount on a medium-sized item after some friendly bargaining.

• If you think the shopkeeper is asking too much, be willing to pretend that you've completely lost interest in the object and walk away, saying you'll look elsewhere. (He may run after you with a better price!)

• Be patient and enjoy the process! Accept the shopkeeper's offer of coffee or tea, if he makes one, and take the chance to chat about other subjects as well.

• If you agree on a price, or if the shopkeeper drops to a price you've named, stand by your word and purchase the item.

The Novice

Syrian shopkeepers can drive a hard bargain, so don't feel bad if you don't get the price you think you deserve. One night, I wanted to purchase a set of carved chess pieces for my sister before she left Damascus, but after an hour of bargaining and a cup of tea I still ended up paying several dollars more than the advertised price in another shop nearby! My mistake? The other shop had unexpectedly closed for the evening, and this shopkeeper had probably heard me say to my sister as we came in that I was determined to buy her this set tonight and not look any further or risk not being able to make the purchase before we left the city. Feigned indifference can be a powerful tool, but it wasn't one available to me.

CULTURAL LIFE

An important concept for understanding the nexus between "high culture" and politics in Syria is that of *tanfiis*, which, lacking an exact single-word translation, means "letting out air" or "making someone breathe." This refers to the process by which the authorities manage discontent by allowing some cultural events that are politically critical, which are thought to siphon off popular discontent. If you keep the lid on a full pot of water over a high flame, it'll eventually boil over unless you open the lid a crack. Cultural productions such as movies, books, and films can offer a similar sort of release for the tension built up by everyday frustrations—whether via humor or by suggesting a sense of solidarity with fictional characters who suffer through similar travails. The more rarefied a cultural medium is—that is, the fewer the people who take an interest in it—the more politically critical it can be. Thus, theater can be more overtly critical than television, and highbrow literature more than newspapers.

Cinema

The tragedy of Syrian cinema is that while it has produced some beautiful works, these films tend to be extremely difficult for anyone, including those who worked on them, to get hold of or view. Most Syrian films are funded by a National Cinema Foundation that keeps its fist tightly clenched around these movies, rarely permitting them to be screened and occasionally even banning films that it itself provided the money for! The Syrian film industry makes only a few feature-length titles each year, but they are typically of much higher quality than what emerges from Egypt, the Middle East's traditional film center.

One Syrian movie that's more widely available on the world market and worth watching for its social and political satire is *The Borders*, featuring the well-known Syrian comic Dureid Lehham as a hapless traveler who loses his passport between border stations and is forced to build a new life on the line between two countries, no longer able to fully enter either one. Another movie that's not often screened, but which should not be missed if you have a chance to see it in Syria, is Nabil al-Malih's moving *The Extras*, about a young couple's difficulty finding the time and space to be alone together.

Literature

Reading is not a popular pastime in Syria, like most of the rest of the Middle East; an oft-repeated joke has it that Arabic-language books are written in Egypt, published in Lebanon, smuggled through Syria, and read in Iraq. Indeed, the Syrian government does ban certain works, but many bookstores stock them behind the counters anyway—since these bans naturally make the books more popular than they would have been otherwise.

Nonetheless, some great names in modern Arabic literature have emerged from the Syrian milieu. Foremost among them is the poet Adonis (pen name of Ali Ahmed Said), whose radical critique of Arab culture has earned him both admirers and enemies, and the poet Nizar Qabbani, whose love poetry is a popular favorite. The playwright Sa'adallah Wannous's expansive repertoire and insistence that Arabs are "condemned to hope" made him an important literary voice, if sometimes a didactic one, and among novelists, Hanna Mina's tales of the sea stand out. Zakaria Tamer is a blacksmith-turned-prolific-writer of allegorical short stories, and the playwright, poet, novelist, and screenwriter Mohammad al-Maghout is perhaps most famous for his collection of essays called *I Will Betray My Country*, whose bitter satire of the Arab political scene still rings true two decades later.

TELEVISION

In contrast to the film industry, with its production of a few unknown movies every year, the dramatic serials that come out of the fecund Syrian television scene are broadcast and loved across the Middle

East; one of these shows, *Bab al-Hara* (The Neighborhood's Gate), was recently estimated to be one of the ten most-watched TV shows in the world. Syrian TV shows are typically produced in units of around thirty installments, because they often premier during Ramadan, with one episode aired every day of the monthlong holiday. They come in several genres, such as social realism (in which characters work through surprisingly realistic conflicts with family, friends, and society); nostalgia (shows like *Bab al-Hara*, which show a romantic version of life in the early twentieth century); biopics (dramatizing the life of a famous person); and classical historical dramas (which focus on heroes or events of classical Arabic culture).

Another recent television phenomenon in Syria is the Turkish soap operas that are dubbed into Syrian Arabic: their popularity has reached heights previously unheard of and even spawned a rush of Arab tourists to the sites where they were filmed. These shows were a flop in Turkey, where few people have seen or heard of them, but in Syrian markets you can see plenty of T-shirts and other paraphernalia featuring the faces of the main actors.

MUSIC

Most of the great names in Arabic music are from an older generation, the most popular of whom is probably Fairuz, the Lebanese singer whose voice is considered an indispensable part of any morning routine; her son Ziad ar-Rahbani is also a popular, and more modern, singer and songwriter. Several

Egyptian singers, such as the late, great Um Kulthoum and Abel Halim Hafez, are popular as well. This sort of classical Arabic music coexists easily with the Arab pop artists followed mostly by young people, like Amr Diab and Nancy Ajram. Some Syrians also enjoy Western pop artists. Music is an important part of gatherings, from picnics to weddings, and if there's no CD player or radio around Syrians won't hesitate to produce their own music by singing and clapping to keep the beat.

DANCE

Although attending professional dance performances isn't something most Syrians do, popular dance is nonetheless integrated into many parts of Syrian life. No large gathering is complete without at least one rendition—more likely many—of the *debke*, a circular folk dance with regional variations. One of the dance's simple beauties is that everyone can participate: linking hands, participants form a line of potentially infinite length led by a dancer who performs more complex movements, and repeat a few basic steps as the line moves in a counterclockwise circle.

Men and women also have distinct styles of dancing to modern pop tunes, with women performing the difficult undulations known popularly in the West as "belly dancing," while men raise their arms in the air and move their hips more gently. Conservative women may prefer not to dance in front of non-related men, but dance is a staple of all-women gatherings, a fun way to move as well as a chance to show off one's agility and skills to the mothers of potential husbands.

BARS AND NIGHTCLUBS

Restaurants and cafés often serve both food and alcohol; after dinner they may be transformed into drinking venues offering beer, wine, and *araq* (but rarely mixed drinks). Establishments that serve only alcohol are not as common. The Middle East is stereotyped as a dry region, but as we've seen, many Syrian minorities as well as nonreligious Muslims do drink, and the alcohol consumption in these nightspots can be prodigious. Public drunkenness is illegal, so be careful about displaying your intoxication.

There aren't many nightclubs in Syria, but those that exist aren't too different from clubs in the West, getting started late and ending early in the morning. Both men and women should dress up when going out to a club, but girls who want to wear something revealing would do well to don a long jacket on the walk there or take a taxi straight to the door.

SPORTS

Sports are a popular pastime for children and teenagers, and although soccer is by far the most popular, basketball also has its fans. Less widespread but still present are swimming, track and field, and tennis. Syria has many club soccer teams and national men and women's soccer teams, but these don't usually fare especially well on the international scene. Even Syrians who don't actively play soccer tend to be avid spectators, attending local matches, watching national games on TV, and following international matches with interest even if their home team isn't playing. If you like soccer, too, say so—it's a great way to bond.

DAY TRIPS

Urban Syrians are always eager to get away on weekends, and Friday is a popular day for outings, whether to a green picnic area, to the village from which one's family hails, or to a local tourist site such as the great Crusader castle Krak des Chevaliers. If they can muster a large enough group, people often rent buses or microbuses with a driver for the purpose. These excursions typically last all day, as destinations may be several hours away and it is uncommon for such groups to stay overnight in hotels.

The long bus ride isn't considered a waste of time when trekking to far-off locations; instead, it is considered an integral part of the trip, and sometimes the most fun part of all! You'll rarely find a Syrian who wastes a bus ride sitting and staring out the window; they're more likely to stand up to dance, drum, and sing. After they've arrived, similar activities are the order of the day. People usually bring packed lunches, or less commonly eat in the restaurants strategically placed in scenic locations.

MUST-SEE SIGHTS
In Damascus

A history buff could spend years exploring the world's oldest city and never get bored. But if you only have a few days, be sure to visit:

Ummayad Mosque: set on a site that's been a place of worship for thousands of years, the

sweeping expanse of the Ummayad Mosque dates
back to the eighth century CE, and the grandeur of
its clean lines and marble fixtures manages to be
both imposing and peaceful at once. A shrine inside
the prayer hall is said to contain the head of John
the Baptist. The mosque is still in use, not a mere
historic relic, so you'll find families relaxing in the
courtyard and praying inside. Don't let your shoes
touch the floor if you're carrying them, and don't
walk directly in front of, or distract, anyone praying.

Shrine of Sayyida Ruqayya: The decoration inside
this Iranian-funded Shia' mosque and shrine of
Sayyida Ruqayya, daughter of the Prophet
Muhammad's son-in-law Ali, is almost unparalleled
in Syria (the exception being another Iranian-built
mosque, that of Sayyida Zeinab), with every inch
of the walls and ceiling covered by either intricate
geometric mosaics or cut mirrors. Many of the
visitors are Iranian pilgrims, and the atmosphere
inside often reaches a fever pitch as the devout are
overcome by the sight of the mausoleum.

Turkish bath: Not all Syrians go to the *hammam*
(public baths), since running water has made them

unnecessary for practical purposes, but some still attend them once in a while to relax or prepare for special occasions like weddings. Don't hesitate to pay extra to have someone else scrub you: an invigorating and pleasurable experience.

Al-Azem Palace: Perhaps representing the apex of surviving Damascene architecture, al-Azem Palace is a cultural museum housed in the former residence of the al-Azem family, which governed Syria during the eighteenth century. Although the displays don't invite one to linger, the beautiful decoration in the rooms they're housed in certainly does.

Naranj: This restaurant, located on Straight Street, is generally thought to be Damascus's best, and President al-Assad is known to have invited foreign dignitaries here. Nevertheless, at around 1,000–1,500 SP per person, it remains extremely affordable for Western visitors (foreign exchange rates permitting!). Be sure to try the dishes that are marked as Naranj specialties—they're what really make the restaurant stand out.

Outside Damascus

Bosra: Combining the most impressive part of two eras, Bosra's central attraction is its enormous Roman amphitheater situated inside a citadel from the early Islamic period.

Palmyra: Probably the most splendid Roman ruins in the Middle East, as well as the base of the rebellious Queen Zenobia in the fourth century CE.

Krak des Chevaliers: An incredibly well preserved and restored Crusader castle. Allow hours to explore its passageways—and bring a flashlight!

Old City and citadel of Aleppo: The enormous castle and labyrinthine Old City market of Aleppo are in better condition and considerably more impressive than those of Damascus; they're best enjoyed with a few hours to spare.

Dead Cities: These towns have remained impressively intact since they were abandoned almost fifteen hundred years ago. You won't be able to visit all six hundred, but one or two make a wonderful day trip out of Aleppo, especially in pleasant weather that will allow you to enjoy the stark and rocky beauty of the surrounding hillsides.

chapter seven

TRAVEL, HEALTH, & SAFETY

Traveling around Syria can be frustrating at times. If you go by car, you may find the local driving style a bit more chaotic than you're used to, and if you travel by public transportation, it'll be characterized by crowding and unexpected delays. Syrians take these holdups in stride and you would do well to emulate them. The transportation infrastructure is generally good, if basic; buses and trains run regularly, but amenities both on board and at stations are few. If you're picky, use the bathroom before you travel and bring your own sustenance, or you'll be left with little but candy and fast food to choose from (like airplanes, however, Syrian buses serve water on board). Palpable rewards do come with the frustrations: not only are the historical sights both well preserved and beautiful, but your fellow Syrian travelers are invariably pleasant, patient, and ready to help.

ROADS AND TRAFFIC

Syrian roads may not be the craziest in the world, but the lack of attention to familiar traffic laws is virtually guaranteed to intimidate Western travelers: turning signals, lane lines, signs, speed limits, and traffic lights are often ignored, and pedestrians may cross the streets at any point, weaving in and out of traffic. However, this element of unpredictability means that Syrians tend to be good drivers who pay close attention to their surroundings, because they are unable to make assumptions about what other drivers will do. Increasing congestion in the cities, while frustrating, means that many collisions take place at low speeds and do only slight to moderate damage. Furthermore, a recent government campaign to improve motor safety by imposing strict fines for traffic violations and for failing to wear one's seat belt has been surprisingly successful in forcing a few changes on grudging drivers.

Intercity highways are more dangerous due to the high speeds at which cars travel; they also frequently lack appropriate nighttime lighting. Therefore, even more than the usual caution should be exercised when driving at night.

LOCAL TRANSPORTATION
Microbuses

A midsized van that seats twelve people comfortably, the microbus (called a *servees* in Arabic) is an efficient way to travel both within cities and between them. In town, these travel on fixed routes announced by a lighted sign on the roof. Since the *servees* signs are only in Arabic, riding them may be difficult for visitors who don't read the script; however, if you have a destination in mind, it is possible to simply inquire until you find the right microbus and hop on.

Fares vary, but the most common official fare is 9 SP, which is almost always rounded up to 10 SP because of the scarcity of single-pound coins. There are no tickets for microbuses. If you're sitting near the front of the vehicle, hand your fare directly to the driver; otherwise, give it to other passengers to pass on to him. Drivers will give you change, but only to a point—don't try to pay for one person with a 500 SP bill.

Despite the government effort aimed at inducing the microbuses to pick up passengers only at designated stops, it remains common practice to flag down the *servees* at any point along its route by raising one's arm, and the driver will usually stop unless his van is already full—or if there's a policeman watching. If he doesn't stop, don't worry; on busy routes, several microbuses might pass by in a minute. The driver usually tries to squeeze as many people as possible into the van, with two people in the front seat next to him, and several people crouching in the narrow, right-hand aisle. It's not acceptable for a woman to sit in the front seat unless accompanied by a man she knows, or to sit on the floor.

Passengers can get off the *servees* at any point in the route by asking the driver to pull over, for which a number of phrases are serviceable, such as *Nizzilni huun, iza bitreed* ("Let me down, please").

Buses
Some Syrian cities also have a system of large green public buses that function much like the microbuses, with a few key differences: they come

by less frequently, are slower, and generally pick up passengers at designated stops—three-sided, clear plastic kiosks with benches. They also require tickets to ride, which are 10 SP each and can be bought from the bus driver. The ticket must be validated by inserting it into the machine located just inside the door at the front, which clips a corner and stamps it.

Taxis

Syria's yellow taxis are only loosely regulated, so agreeing on the right fare can be a challenge, but they are still a faster, if more expensive, alternative to the microbus system, and are the best option for non-Arabic speakers or anyone in a hurry. Most cabs have meters, but prices tend to be negotiable. Taxis are common and easy to flag down in most  cities; at rush hour, though, it's a good idea to check with the driver *before* climbing in to see if he's willing to travel to your destination, which he may legitimately refuse. The same applies if you're going on a farther-than-normal trip or if it's late at night. It can also be a good idea to ask the driver whether or not he has a working meter, unless you already have a good idea of a fair price for your destination or are up for a round of bargaining. If you're not sure how much your trip should cost, check with a Syrian or two beforehand. Once in the taxi, it's polite for men to take the front seat next to the driver, but women should never do so since it could be interpreted as a sexual invitation.

TAXIS: A FAIR FARE

- Unless you're happy to haggle, check to see if there's a working meter before getting in.

- If there's a meter, check the starting price; the most recently adjusted meters begin at 5.50 SP (as of this writing), while older ones begin at 5.00 SP and don't rise as rapidly.

- At the end of the trip, add some 5–25 SP to the value on a newer meter, and even more if it's an older one. This isn't really an optional tip, but rather a "cost of living" increase in the fare.

- Just how much you add is relative; consider just 5 SP or rounding up for a fare of 20–30 SP, or 25 if the meter reads more like 100–150 SP.

- If the driver failed to turn on the meter at the beginning, or took an extra-long route, then you might legitimately give him only the metered amount (or even less for real skullduggery).

- After midnight, drivers won't turn on their meters and may legitimately charge higher rates (at least a normal fare and a half), which should be negotiated beforehand.

- Bear in mind that taxi driving is a low-status, poorly paying job whose practitioners struggle to make ends meet, so it's best to err on the side of generosity.

The Benefit of the Doubt

Taxi drivers who don't turn on the meter aren't necessarily untrustworthy! Once an American student in Aleppo hailed a cab and asked to be taken to the bus station. The taxi driver suggested a flat fee, which the student refused, demanding to pay by the meter. The taxi driver acquiesced—and the student was dismayed to see that the final reading on the meter was more than the price initially asked for.

Walking

Most Syrian cities have an active street life, and walkers are common. Pedestrians tend to cross the road anywhere since there are few designated crosswalks, while drivers, who expect this behavior and resent it, don't always slow down until the last minute. If you're faced with the prospect of crossing an unusually busy and daunting street, look for a Syrian doing the same and follow their movements. Drivers usually consider themselves to have the right-of-way and may interpret waving or making eye contact as your acknowledgment of this fact; instead, keep a careful but stone-faced watch out of the corner of your eye as you cross.

INTERCITY TRAVEL

Planes

Both the state-run Syrian Air and the private Syrian Pearl airlines connect Damascus with Aleppo, Deir az-Zor, and Qamishli on a daily basis. For most Syrians, flying between cities is an unaffordable luxury.

Coaches and Microbuses

Both coaches and microbuses travel between Syrian cities. The coach service connects the larger cities, while microbuses move between regional hubs and their outlying towns and villages. Coach tickets do not need to be bought more than an hour ahead of time, except on major holidays; microbuses, of course, don't take tickets, so you'll pay after boarding.

Coach rides can be noisy, with music, Egyptian movies, or Syrian TV shows playing; bring earplugs if you plan to sleep. However, they will probably be clean, comfortable, and serve water throughout the trip. Bus seats are often assigned to ensure that unaccompanied men and women aren't seated next to each other. Some Syrians may want to strike up a conversation, in which case you should respond politely, but it's also acceptable to remain silent if no one makes an effort to talk. Long bus rides usually include a fifteen-minute rest stop where you can use the bathroom or purchase candy, tea, coffee, or simple fast food.

Trains

There is a rail service connecting many cities in Syria, but it is generally less popular than buses because it is considerably slower, although it can be cheaper. First and second class are available, but even first has few amenities.

Hitchhiking

Hitchhiking is not common and is mainly practiced by foreigners, although Syrians used to hitch lifts more frequently, before bus services crisscrossed the country. It is no more dangerous than anywhere else, but women should never hitchhike alone.

WHERE TO STAY
Hotels

All manner of hotels are available in Syria, from backpacker hostels to the fancy Four Seasons and Cham Palace in Damascus, and prices range accordingly from a few dollars a night to hundreds. Recently a number of boutique hotels have been established in the restored houses of Damascus's Old City, and while all are undeniably beautiful, not all are of the same quality: some have been carefully restored using traditional techniques, while other developers have used cheap materials inappropriate for the architecture, or pushed the structure beyond what it should accommodate—

building with cement rather than wood and mud bricks, for instance, and adding too many bathrooms. The choice of hotels outside the major population centers is considerably more limited.

Although many hotels offer good service, Syria's undeveloped and nonstandardized tourist infrastructure means that a few words of caution are in order. First of all, some hoteliers can be tricky when working with different currencies, so ask ahead of time what exchange rate they're using or how much exactly they charge in dollars, euros, pounds, or whatever you prefer to pay in—and get it in writing. Secondly, not all hotels have backup generators—especially the cheaper ones or those outside Damascus—so bring a flashlight in case the electricity fails, which happens daily in some areas.

Apartments

For anyone planning to stay a while, apartments are widely available for rent in Damascus, and prices vary wildly depending on the size and location. The most expensive are in Damascus's manicured, centrally located neighborhoods, while outlying conurbations are less expensive—the farther from the center, the cheaper.

There are several ways to find an apartment. One method is simply to wander around a neighborhood asking shopkeepers if there are any vacancies nearby—they usually know the local residents and can introduce you to potential landlords. A more efficient but also more costly method is to employ a *simsar*, or real estate agent, who will be able to show you a number of possibilities at once. The *simsar* won't ask for any payments before you decide on a place, but he'll take a large fee when you do, usually half of the first month's rent.

There are a few things you should ask about before you rent an apartment. First, rules about couples: some landlords refuse to rent to male-and-female roommate combinations without a marriage certificate, and other landlords will object to you having guests of the opposite sex over. Second, taxes and registration fees: foreigners who want to apply for residency must sign an apartment contract and register it at the *muhafiza*, or local government office. However, many landlords prefer not to do this because it means that they will pay higher taxes, and they may request that the tenants compensate them for this if they insist on registering. Third, utilities: they may or may not be included in the rent. Lastly, heating: the most

common method of warming a
place is with a *sobiya*, or diesel
stove, while some apartments
merely have electric heaters and
a very few have central heating.
Each of these options comes
with separate costs that the
renter should be prepared to
bear; but having some type
of heat source is important as
Syrian apartments are not
well insulated.

Renting Rooms

Many of the traditional Arab-style houses in
Damascus's Old City have vacant rooms, and a
popular way for landlords to make some extra
money is to rent them out to both Syrian and
foreign students. It's easy to find them, by asking
shopkeepers, by knocking on doors and inquiring if
there are any rooms for rent, or by looking around
for flyers. Since many families still live in these
homes, it's important to ask about the relationship
they have with their tenants: some treat their renters
like part of the family and expect them to follow all
the rules of the house, such as observing a curfew
and not bringing over guests, while others are
satisfied with regular payments and don't want to
act as chaperones. If there are a number of foreign
students sharing part or all of the house, ask one or
two about the environment—is it cooperative or
solitary, clean or messy, quiet or raucous? Some all-
foreigner houses are the sites of wild parties on the
weekends, so make sure you know what you're
getting into if that's not your ideal atmosphere.

HEALTH
Preparing for Your Visit

Before you travel to Syria, make sure your routine vaccinations are in order, in addition to shots for hepatitis A and B, typhoid, and rabies (if you will be working with animals or doing a lot of outdoor activities; stray dogs are rare in Syrian cities). If you need any special medications, bring enough for the duration of your trip. Bring some powdered Gatorade with you in case of traveler's diarrhea, since such electrolyte-replacing drinks aren't available on every street corner in Syria—you may not need it, but you'll be happy to have it if you do. It is recommended that you take out travel insurance to protect you from situations ranging from lost luggage to emergency medical evacuation.

Syria is generally a safe country that poses few unusual health risks, but take commonsense precautions to ward off irritations like mosquitoes and sunstroke. It can be very hot in the summer, so stay hydrated and carry bottled water with you at all times.

Hospitals and Medical Care

Medical care at public hospitals and clinics is free for Syrians, but foreigners don't qualify for this and will not be admitted to these facilities except in a life-threatening emergency. Instead, they pay cash on a per-procedure basis at the country's many private clinics and hospitals, which are generally considered to be of a higher quality. Enough asking around can usually produce a doctor who has studied medicine abroad and speaks a foreign language fluently;

some embassy Web sites also list such physicians. Syrian doctors are generally competent, and health care is extremely affordable compared to countries like the United States, but even private hospitals don't always have the resources for the latest equipment and techniques. Hence, it's better to save major surgical and other procedures for elsewhere. Health facilities in rural areas tend to be more poorly equipped than in the cities.

STAYING HYDRATED

Most Syrian homes have two faucets, one for drinking water and one for nondrinking water. The drinking-water faucet is usually referred to as "*the fijeh*" after the spring that is the source of much of this water, and while it is typically turned on from about 5:00 a.m. to 2:00 p.m., these times vary from neighborhood to neighborhood. Those staying in hotels should buy bottled water to drink—they're available at nearly every food stand and convenience store, so it's not necessary to bring water-purification tablets or filters.

Hygiene When Eating Out

The vast majority of restaurants in Syria do not observe Western standards of cleanliness in food preparation. Kitchen workers don't wear gloves or hairnets, and when food stands are manned by a single employee, he takes the money with the same hand that dishes out the meals. Most Syrian restaurants and food stands are safe to eat in, however; the best way to tell is to see which have a lot of Syrian patrons. For foreigners used to Western food, some stomach upset is normal soon after arriving in Syria, simply due to the change in diet. Should the sickness prove serious or long-lasting, drugs are easily available over the counter at pharmacies.

SAFETY
Terrorism and Crime
Although Syria is often portrayed in the Western press as a "state sponsor of terrorism," it is in reality an extremely safe country for foreigners. Terrorist attacks by fringe Islamist groups are extremely rare and crime rates are very low in comparison to Western countries—particularly violent crime. Pickpocketing and petty theft is an occasional danger, so it's a good idea to keep one's valuables close by, but in general the combination of an omnipresent police force and closely knit communities means that the traveler, or resident, has little to fear. If you do happen to be the victim of a serious crime, however, you should report it to the police and your embassy.

Sexual Harassment
While the harassment of women is becoming a significant problem in some Middle Eastern countries, it remains at relatively low levels in Syria. Nonetheless, harassment does exist, and the extent to which it rears its ugly head can vary not only from region to region but also from neighborhood to neighborhood in the same city. The harassment is usually verbal, ranging from inane platitudes like "Welcome-how-are-you?" to lewd innuendos, although groping does occasionally occur as well.

Harassment of women is an expression of the patriarchal social system in Syria—of male control of both women and public space—and is a complex issue even on the most practical level. Some women find it upsetting and threatening; others claim that it is a gratifying form of attention. Many men see it as a harmless pastime, even an outlet for creativity. Wearing conservative clothing does not safeguard against unwanted attention, as even Syrian women who dress modestly may be tormented.

On the other hand, it is undeniable that dressing in overly revealing clothes does increase the likelihood of harassment; Syrian women do not usually wear tank tops, low-cut shirts, midriff-revealing tops, shorts, or short skirts on the street, and visitors would do well to emulate them. Foreign women should bear in mind that perceptions of Western women are filtered through images that reach Syria via the American media, specifically the film industry, in which the typical female character's behavior is licentious by Syrian standards, so a short skirt on a foreign woman in public can send a powerful message. (Blond women, furthermore, are sometimes mistaken for Russian "hookers," although this usually doesn't result in much more than a verbal overture.)

Harassment of women is a crime in Syria, and although women don't commonly resort to law and prosecute their tormentors, this does occur and is an option for foreigners as well. More simply, shouting for help on the street often brings passersby to one's aid. Women tend to develop their own responses according to their comfort levels. Effeminate-looking men are occasionally harassed as well, although this is much less common.

chapter eight

BUSINESS BRIEFING

THE BUSINESS LANDSCAPE

Under the socialist Ba'ath Party, Syria's economy was long centralized and state-dominated; the country is now in the midst of a slow economic opening up to foreign investment, increased imports, and privatization. The new model has been christened a "social market economy." This process has been underway for over a decade, but is far from complete, so Syria presents a considerable untapped market and a wealth of unexploited business opportunities—as well as significant challenges for investors and entrepreneurs, who must be prepared to deal with the slowness and inefficiencies that are a legacy of the state-run economy and its accompanying enormous bureaucracy.

There's certainly an illiberal side to economic reform as well: small and mid-level businesspeople may operate with some independence from the government, but government and business are tightly intertwined at the very highest levels, since the old elite—especially those with preexisting government connections—have been some of the biggest beneficiaries of private development contracts. Privatization has also sped ahead of the development of a good legal climate for business.

A Syrian magazine that once attempted to rank the country's hundred richest businessmen admitted that due to a lack of transparency it simply couldn't do it, opting to list those it thought wealthiest in alphabetical order instead.

Businesses in Syria range from the very large and professionally run, like the cell phone carriers (MTN and Syriatel), to small- and medium-sized family businesses where leadership is inherited and decision making is a family affair. The vast majority fall into this latter category, so foreign businesspeople must be prepared to take family dynamics, as well as purely business concerns, into account.

A Note on American Sanctions

Syria is subject to a web of unilateral American sanctions that can be a hassle for Americans wanting to do business with or in the country. Most importantly, the 2003 Syria Accountability and Lebanese Sovereignty Restoration Act prohibits the export of US goods to Syria (with the exception of food and medicine), forbids US business to operate in Syria, prohibits Syrian airlines from flying to the USA, and restricts the movement of Syrian diplomats in the USA. The stated reasons for the law include encouraging Syria to cease a number of activities: the stationing of its armed forces in Lebanon (an objective achieved in 2005, though not by the sanctions); the support of Hezbollah and Palestinian factions such as Hamas; the development of biological, chemical, or nuclear weapons; and cooperation with the movement of arms and militants into Iraq. Some organizations and individuals in Syria are also affected by Executive Order 13224 of 2001 ("Blocking Terrorist Property"), Executive Order 13338 of 2004 (with many of the same provisions as the Syria Accountability Act, allowing also for the freezing of some individuals' assets), Executive Order 13460 of 2008 (blocking the property of individuals connected to public corruption in Syria), and the Iran and Syria Nonproliferation Act of 2005 (placing sanctions on certain companies and organizations). Additionally, the Syrian participation in the boycott of Israeli products conflicts with US antiboycott policies. Hence, businesspeople interested in conducting business in Syria would do well to consult a legal expert.

BUSINESS CULTURE
Importance of Personal Relations
The key to business success in Syria is widely acknowledged to lie in connections and relationships, a category that covers both familial relations and friendships. Connections define not only who obtains work in which company, but are also of the utmost importance in forming business partnerships and getting almost anything done.

Syrians feel that having a personal relationship with a fellow businessman or woman not only makes problems easier to resolve, without having to go through slow official channels, but is also a form of insurance against bad practices. If you don't know a businessperson or contractor, the thinking goes, how can you be sure that he won't cheat after a deal is signed, or charge an unfair price? Better to deal with someone who's already known to you.

Foreign businesspeople should certainly attempt to build good relationships with the Syrians they work with, but luckily for them relationships do not necessarily play as important a role in their success and acceptance, since they're considered to come bearing significant experience or capital, or both. While foreign expertise is a good starting point for a business relationship, however, you should definitely spend time building on it to form a relationship of mutual trust and regard.

Business Structures

As we have seen, many Syrian businesses are family run, and the demands of the business sometimes play second fiddle to the demands of family dynamics with regard to who makes decisions and when tasks are completed. Family members usually form the company's board of directors, with the family patriarch as chairman. What's important for foreign businesspeople to understand, however, is that it's not the patriarch but his sons or grandsons who will be the easiest and most effective members of the family to deal with—they're more likely to speak foreign languages, understand the West, and possess a strong sense of entrepreneurship. As long as you don't downright ignore the older generation of the family, which is likely to have the final say in decisions, it's fine to concentrate on the younger ones—they're still an integral part of the decision-making process. Family dynamics may also influence what business ventures appeal to a family-owned company: a religious Muslim family is unlikely to take part in importing beer, for example, no matter how big the potential market.

Time
Business works at a much slower pace in Syria in comparison not only to Western countries but also to other Arab countries that have moved further along in the process of economic liberalization. This is partly due to the particular style of Syrian business, which emphasizes sticking to subordinate–boss relationships and not overstepping the boundaries of a defined role, and partly to the sometimes interminable-seeming paperwork required to clear any step that a business takes with the Syrian government. Government offices are generally not computerized, so all procedures require reams of paperwork with stamps from various departments, and the lack of a single document or stamp can hold up the processing of a file. It is wise to allow more time than officially planned in order to complete a project.

Syrian meetings or events do not typically start precisely on time, but since foreigners are well-known for valuing punctuality, businesspeople will often make an effort to be on time when they know that foreigners are involved. It is thus wise to assume that meetings and other engagements *will* start on time, and to call ahead if you'll be late; at the same time, resign yourself to the fact that not everyone will necessarily follow the same standard and proceedings may start late anyway. Meetings may easily run over time, and appointments that are somewhat social in nature, such as a business lunch or visit to a colleague's home, can consume several hours. Given these facts, it's better not to plan too many engagements for one day or schedule them too closely together.

For large businesses, such as the national phone carriers, working hours run from 9:00 a.m. to 5:00 p.m., Sunday through Thursday, and are usually observed. Government agencies are open from 9:00 a.m. to 3:00 p.m. on the same days, though employees may leave earlier. Small, informal businesses often have a different schedule—opening in midmorning, closing in midafternoon for several hours, and opening up again in the early evening, every day except the holy day of the proprietor (Friday for Muslims, Sunday for Christians).

Business Etiquette

Personal appearance is important, so dress in formal, dark-colored business suits with ties (for men) for all business occasions, including lunches and dinners out. Even if the occasion turns out to be less formal than you'd imagined, you will not lose face by overdressing, while you would certainly show both a lack of respect and a lack of self-worth by dressing too casually. Syrian businesspeople follow Western norms in business dress, so a visit to Syria doesn't require any significant changes in wardrobe, though women should take care to dress modestly.

Syrians frequently exchange business cards, so it's good to have a large stack of your own on hand at all times. They sometimes put more contact information on their cards—such as personal cell phone numbers and e-mail addresses—than Westerners do, but it's fine to provide only your business contact information if that's an effective way to reach you; conversely, don't hesitate to reach a business contact on his or her personal cell phone if that's the number you were given.

It's both good manners and good sense to pay personal attention to one's business contacts; people with whom you've built up a good relationship can make life easier by recommending others they trust, pulling strings, or guiding you through official channels, and simply enriching your understanding of Syrian culture and business practices. It is rude to treat others simply as a source of information or funding, or as just one end of a business deal; while in some countries confining discussions with a business partner to work might be taken as a sign of respect for their time and expertise, in Syria it could be seen as cold and distant. Here, *saving* time isn't money; *investing* time in a business relationship can be. Take care to get to know your partners' background and interests, and to ask regularly about their health and that of their family. This is, of course, more appropriate in some contexts than others—a little chitchat works well before a meeting, while more in-depth conversations can take place during a meal out or a visit to someone's home. Don't refuse these social invitations—they're an important part of a business relationship and provide a great chance to get to know your partners better.

MEETINGS

When you enter a meeting, begin by greeting everyone there, starting with the most senior person—usually the oldest. If you know or suspect that the family is religious, don't initiate handshakes with people of the opposite sex; if they feel comfortable, the other party can initiate them. Otherwise, greet people with eye contact, a smile, and your right hand over your heart. Businessmen may hug each other in greeting after they've formed a close relationship. The seating arrangement isn't important and won't tell you much about the seniority of the people present, but clothing can: if anyone in the room is in casual dress, then he or she is a low-level assistant or technician, not a key decision maker.

Meetings usually begin with an address by the boss or person in charge, during which ordinary employees are reluctant to interrupt or comment without  having been given permission. After a topic has been opened to general discussion, however, meetings can become free-for-alls where anyone can speak out, even if it involves cutting others off. People will take cell phone calls during meetings and smoke, and it would be rude to request that cigarettes be put out. This seemingly chaotic style means that meetings can easily run longer than expected, so it's a good idea to make appointments widely spaced, and to approach them with patience and good humor. Deviations into side topics don't mean that the matter at hand won't be completed, only that the meeting isn't proceeding in a totally linear fashion.

One of the challenges you may face during business meetings, particularly with representatives of family businesses, is striking a balance in your dealings with the different generations. As mentioned previously, it will be easier to interact with the younger members of the family, but don't forget to acknowledge the importance of the older family members present.

Syrians are often happy to hone and display their English and their hospitality by conducting meetings entirely in English when foreigners are present, but unless their language skills are unusually strong they may resort to Arabic if trickier subjects come up. Furthermore, not all Syrians have had the same opportunities to develop their language skills, so an interpreter can be useful—something that's also true if you prefer to conduct business in a language other than English, which is the second language of choice in Syria.

PRESENTATIONS

Presentations are increasingly common, although the styles vary greatly depending on who is presenting. For foreigners, the cultural and language barrier between Syrian and Western businesspeople means that even if a translator is present, it's important to include charts and graphics to clarify key concepts and plans. Presentations should be well organized, which shows competence; dress and presentation style should be formal and serious. It's best to steer clear of jokes, which may be lost in translation and either unintentionally offend or merely fall flat. If you don't like being interrupted, specify that your presentation is meant to be informative, not a discussion, and that you'll leave time at the end for questions; otherwise, expect to be interrupted with questions and comments throughout.

NEGOTIATIONS

Syrians love to negotiate; they see it as an art form and almost an end in itself, so they're likely to enjoy the negotiations even if they don't succeed in changing the final price much. In Syria, negotiations are something to be savored, and may stretch over many sessions. Syrians are also aggressive negotiators, however, who tend to bid very high or very low at first; you should do the same, and expect your price to undergo significant changes through the process. Since negotiating is an important skill on which Syrians pride themselves, the main decision makers will usually attend in person to engage in the bargaining.

Although foreign businesspeople are seen as having expertise in overseas business practices, they are certainly not seen as experts on Syrian industry, marketing, or national standards, something that smart Syrian businessmen naturally try to exploit in order to get the best deal during negotiations. As such, negotiations are a good time to demonstrate one's own expertise by asking detailed, informed questions. As with meetings, digressions are normal, so don't worry if the discussion doesn't stay on topic all of the time.

Syrians take negotiating quite seriously even outside the realm of business: the former president Hafez al-Asad's stamina in meetings with foreign diplomats was legendary, and he was fond of negotiating for nine or ten hours at a time. He even engaged in what was sometimes called "bladder diplomacy," during which he would serve endless rounds of tea and coffee while drawing out discussions so as to force his opponent to concede his point just to be able to rise from the table and use the bathroom! Businessmen, luckily, are unlikely to face such tactics—but they should still be aware that the Syrians' commitment to hard bargaining runs deep.

CONTRACTS

Syria's civil law is based on French law, with its extensive civil codes. Ideally, this should mean that it is easy to fall back on the law to cover any eventualities not mentioned in a contract. Practically speaking, resorting to legal arbitration of a contract is a slow and arduous practice. The Doing Business Project ranked Syria 176 out of 183 countries in terms of the ease of enforcing contracts. This is one reason that good personal relationships are so important in the Syrian business environment; working with someone you trust is a far better way to get things done than resorting to legal mechanisms.

Contracts tend not to be viewed as binding on the parties with the same level of precision and attention to detail as in the West, where each word is important and carries legal weight. While Syrians certainly regard themselves as being bound by the spirit or goals of a contract, they do not always view the supporting clauses as carrying the same level of gravity. Putting agreements in writing is particularly important because Syrians may pledge to do things they know that they cannot deliver simply because they feel it would be rude to refuse a request; alternatively, they may make offers that they have little intention of fulfilling because making the offer is in itself a form of social lubrication and a gesture of goodwill. In other cases, of course, they take their given word very seriously, but it's best to have everything in writing to maximize the chances that both parties will clearly understand what's expected.

For legal purposes, the contract should be translated into Arabic, but if you're dealing with parties who understand English, then it's all right to sign an English copy. The translation, however, doesn't necessarily have to be an official or notarized version.

"OILING THE WHEELS"

The public sector in Syria is widely known to suffer from a high degree of corruption. While public corruption in the West tends to occur mainly in the upper echelons of power, in Syria it is present at all levels of governance, and naturally  touches the business world at their many points of intersection. Any small sheaf of paperwork completed at a government office may be accompanied by a small bribe, often under US $20, in order to ensure smooth processing and good service on the next visit to the same office. The larger and more important the company and project, of course, the more business and government are likely to be intertwined, and the larger the bribes are likely to be. Foreigners may not be asked to pay bribes personally, but the Syrians they work with will be.

Syrians pay bribes not only when they or their company has done something wrong, but also when they are entirely on the right side of the law, merely in order to ensure a good relationship with low-level government officials. While Syrians universally find the corruption in government disgusting, especially at higher levels, they also sometimes see small bribes as a necessary form of social welfare for low-earning public servants. A government employee who makes the equivalent of only US $200 a month is likely to be in real need of the extra money or gifts he or she receives in the course of daily work in order to put meat rather than bread on the family's table, or present an extra gift to their children on holidays.

FOREIGNERS WORKING IN SYRIA: A FEW TIPS

The Syrian government is somewhat protective of the rights of its own labor force to work, so even though it has greatly eased restrictions on foreign investors and investments in the past few years, foreigners face certain barriers to gaining work visas in Syria. Although it is almost startlingly easy for foreigners to be employed *without* obtaining work permits, particularly if they perform jobs such as teaching English or other foreign languages, it can be a good idea to apply for a work and residency permit if you're involved in a larger, higher-profile project—your Syrian business partners can probably advise you on whether or not it is necessary. Since foreigners who want a work permit must prove that they are better qualified than any Syrian to do the work in question, they must present notarized copies of all diplomas, training certificates, licenses, and other documents that help prove their competence. Hence, it's a good idea to get these documents ready in advance.

WOMEN AND WORK

Women are increasingly entering the workforce in Syria and expect to be treated as equals, though leadership positions remain male dominated. Educated Syrian men usually have no problem working with women as equals and bosses, but less-educated workers are sometimes resistant to being directed by a woman. Successful Syrian businesswomen include Lina Safwan Ashrafieh, who owns a pharmaceutical company in  Aleppo, and Marwa al-Etouni, who works in soap making. Syria's First Lady, Asma al-Asad, used to work as a hedge fund manager in England; since moving to Syria, she's dedicated part of her time to encouraging young girls to become entrepreneurs.

Foreign men should use caution when forming business relationships with Syrian women, and observe the general rules governing the interaction of Syrian women and foreign men. While conservative businesswomen might consider it inappropriate to go out to lunch with a foreign businessman in order to discuss a deal, others treat such an engagement as a normal part of work and leisure. In general, it is safer to avoid one-on-one engagements with Syrian businesswomen one doesn't know well, and discuss pertinent issues with them in a group setting. Foreign businesswomen will probably be treated with the same respect afforded to foreign businessmen, but should naturally observe the boundaries that apply to dealings with any other Syrian men, such as avoiding unnecessary physical contact and dressing conservatively.

SOCIALIZING FOR BUSINESS

Lunches or dinners out with colleagues or potential business partners are common, and provide an opportunity to expand the personal side of a business relationship. The person who extends the invitation is generally expected to foot the bill, and you're not expected to reciprocate unless the relationship has become more personal than business related.

Don't even broach the idea of drinking wine with the meal unless your host initiates it. Even an observant Muslim might feel it rude to prevent you from drinking with your meal, but would still feel uncomfortable—so the best policy is to abstain.

Topics of Conversation

Some topics of conversation are best avoided, like religion, sexual mores, and criticism of the Syrian government. Syrian social circles are dense, so don't gossip about your other acquaintances—there's a good chance the person you're talking to already knows more about them than you do! It is fine to ask questions about Syrian culture, or to discuss international politics (although expressing support for Israel is generally not advisable), and any number of other topics. Syrians are often eager to learn from foreign businesspeople, but do not appreciate being lectured on how far their business environment has yet to go. Syrian businesspeople are well aware that the private sector is still developing, but they appreciate the changes they've seen in the past few years and see reform as an inevitably slow process.

Gifts

Exchanging small gifts is a common part of a business relationship in Syria, so you may want to bring some small items that are representative of your home country or culture. A preserved local food is often a good choice, as long as it doesn't contain alcohol or pork. It's also important to bring a gift if someone invites you to their home, but it is not necessary to bring anything too fancy—sweets, locally produced or foreign, are always a safe choice.

COMMUNICATING

LANGUAGE

All Syrians speak Arabic, and all who have attended school have learned to read it, and to read it well, since Syria's educational system emphasizes a high degree of competency in the language. Arabic is a "diglossic" language: it contains two distinctive levels of speech, one informal, spoken, and localized, and the other formal, written, and shared across the Arab world. This latter register is referred to as Modern Standard Arabic, and is the language in which the vast majority of books, poetry, newspapers, signs, and classical songs are composed; it is also the language of newscasters, formal speeches, and religious sermons. Although Syrians understand this register well, write with it, and draw on it when discussing intellectual topics such as politics, literature, and the economy, they do not use it in everyday conversation; indeed, attempts to use this register in informal situations such as ordering food or catching up with friends gives the conversation an absurdist, highly amusing flavor. In their daily life, Syrians—and all other Arabs—speak a local dialect that can vary drastically, not only between countries but also between cities, and even between neighborhoods.

Syrians can often tell something about their compatriots' ethnic, regional, or religious origins simply by listening to their accents.

Many other languages are also spoken by minorities of Syrians: among themselves, Armenians speak Armenian, Kurds speak Kurdish, and Turkmen speak Turkmen. The mountain town of Ma'alula and a few nearby villages boast the last known native speakers of Aramaic (the language spoken by Jesus).

Merchants are also learning phrases in Turkish and Farsi to take advantage of the tourist influx that's accompanied the removal of visa requirements for Turks and Iranians to enter Syria, while those who work in tourism or near tourist areas are usually able to communicate in a number of European languages. English, however, is first on the list of the most useful and desirable foreign languages for Syrians to know. Few are fluent, but many know at least a few words, particularly in urban areas. No matter what their level, many welcome the chance to practice what they know! Nonetheless, making an effort to use even a few Arabic words will make a good impression and elicit goodwill, while speaking Arabic well will impress even more. If you'd like to study Arabic in Damascus, two of the most common places are the Language Center at the University of Damascus for beginning through intermediate levels, and the Institut Français du Proche-Orient, which offers training for more advanced students.

USEFUL ARABIC PHRASES

Marhaba	Hello
Keefak?	How are you?
Mneeh/a	Good
Al-hamdullah	Thank God
Inshallah	God willing
Wayn…?	Where is…?
Wayn al-hammam?	Where is the bathroom?
Biddi…	I want…
Biddi ruh a'…	I want to go to…
Ma biddi	I don't want (it)
La	No
Na'm or *ayawah*	Yes
Shukran	Thank you
'Afwan	Excuse me
Iza bitreed	Please.

BODY LANGUAGE

In general, Syrians are more physically reserved
in public than Westerners, particularly women.
Women on their own usually keep their eyes
straight ahead and their faces expressionless,
because gazing directly at a man for too long or
smiling at him is an invitation for him to approach.
Similarly, a demure smile from a woman is polite,
but excessive smiling and laughing during a
conversation with a stranger can be interpreted as
flirting. It's common for men to stare openly at
unaccompanied women or for anyone to stare at
foreigners—such a gaze isn't necessarily hostile;
it may just be an attempt to figure out where
you're from!

Physical affection between men and women in public is inappropriate, even between married couples, and a polite man will never touch a strange woman in public—so shopkeepers often drop change into a woman's hand or hold bills by their corners so that she can take them without any improper physical contact. Foreign men should be similarly careful not to come into accidental contact with Syrian women in a way that could be considered inappropriate. On the other hand, women and men may be openly affectionate with friends of their own sex. It's not uncommon to see men walking hand in hand or arm in arm, a practice that doesn't imply any sort of sexual relationship, only close friendship.

SIGNS NOT WORDS

Some gestures used in Syria are common to Western culture, such as the "thumbs up" sign, but others will be new to the visitor:

- "Wait a minute"—palm up, fingers and thumbs together pointing skyward, moved forward and backward.
- "Check, please"—You can ask for a check in a restaurant by using your flat hand, palm up, to intersect the wrist of your raised other hand.
- "No, thanks"—A head sharply tilted backward, or raised eyebrows accompanied by a click of the tongue, is a sign of refusal.
- "Yes, OK"—Patting one's head or pointing to one's eyes is a less common way of signaling acceptance of a request.

THE MEDIA

Syria's media has long been state controlled, but during the past decade a few licenses have been granted for private television stations, radio stations, and newspapers. While even these outlets can't cross the "red lines" of Syrian politics, they have brought some higher-quality local content and increased choices to the market.

Television

By far the most popular medium for both news and entertainment in Syria is television, especially satellite television; many households keep their set on most of the afternoon and evening. As a format whose consumption can be communal, it's a popular way for families to spend time together. The most popular news channel is the famed Qatar-based Al-Jazeera, while options for entertainment abound, from Syrian and Turkish serialized dramas to Egyptian films, to subtitled American or even Bollywood movies and TV shows to regionally produced music videos and talk shows. The official Syrian channels include a satellite channel called Suriya, as well as a Syrian Drama Channel dedicated to airing Syrian television serials. Syrians may watch these for entertainment and shows with local content, but there are too many other good television stations for the Syrian channels to be the primary source of news.

Radio

Radio is a popular form of entertainment and news for a car commute, and public transportation like buses and microbuses might pipe it in as well—the choice rests with the driver, not the passengers! There are a number of radio channels broadcasting music and news, in addition to the official Radio Damascus.

Print Media

Newspapers and magazines are a less popular way of obtaining information. The local Syrian government-published newspapers—*al-Ba'ath, ath-Thawra, Tishreen, al-Jamaahiir* and *al-Wahda*—aren't considered to be good for much more than packing material; all three report similar, pro-government news and rely heavily on the Syrian Arab News Agency, or SANA, to fill their pages. There are some privately owned newspapers and magazines such as *Baladna* and the English-language magazines *Forward Syria* and *Syria Today*, but none have reputations for breaking news or hard-hitting journalism like Al-Jazeera's.

SERVICES
Telephones

Most homes in Syria have landline telephones, which can be used to make local calls to other landline phones for very little money. Cell phones are also very widespread in Syria, and a new line with one of the two cellular carriers, Syriatel or MTN, can be purchased relatively cheaply (remember to bring your passport when you open the line). Afterward, you can buy prepaid cards to load credits on your phone, just as most Syrians do.

Talking on one's cell phone is relatively expensive, at 9 US cents per minute—there is virtually no difference or competition between the two phone companies—so Syrians tend not to linger on the phone, spending only as long as is necessary to make plans. Syrian phones are only charged for outgoing calls and text messages; those incoming are free. Since most don't have voicemail, it's common to either send a text message or call repeatedly if a call isn't answered the first time. This high cost, and the fact that no one is charged until a call is answered, has spawned a sublanguage of "missed calls," in which users communicate for free by hanging up immediately after they place a call. The recipients, seeing a notice on their phone that they missed a call, might understand from this that the caller is running low on minutes and wants to be called back, or that any number of prearranged signals between friends is being utilized—anything from "I have arrived home safely" to "I'm thinking of you." In this way, even those who can't afford to talk on their cell phones much can still keep one around—the arrangement is useful for many, since they've rapidly become a status symbol.

Mail

As with other government services in Syria, the mail can be a bit erratic. Anything sent from abroad by regular mail stands a good chance of arriving late: one US citizen received her ballot for the US presidential election of November 2008 the following June! Packages or letters sent by registered or priority mail are much more likely to arrive in a timely manner. Since many Syrian apartment buildings and houses do not have clear addresses, it's a good idea to use an institutional address if you have one, or ask your landlord the best way to address a letter.

Packages have to be picked up from the central post office; although you're supposed to get a slip notifying you that a package has arrived, it may not be sent, so it's important to track your package online and go to the post office to pick it up whenever you think it's arrived, bringing your passport as identification. Letters and packages *sent* abroad from the central post office seem to arrive fairly reliably, although they may be opened at customs; some prefer to use more expensive shipping companies such as FedEx. The post office itself is a bureaucracy, but a rather benign one: the office can be chaotic when busy, and around an hour should be allowed for completing any transaction, but people are more than willing to help out if you're confused.

Internet
The Internet is growing in popularity in Syria: although the medium was introduced to the country as recently as 2000, almost a fifth of the population was using it in 2008 and more start all the time. Among urban youth and professionals, of course, that number is much higher, while the Internet is practically nonexistent in rural areas.

The Web is a source of both news and entertainment, but it is subject to government censorship, of both politically sensitive and of popular but largely apolitical Web sites such as

YouTube and Facebook. These blocks are quite easy to get around, and Syrians are adept at using proxy software to do so. Larger barriers to Internet use in Syria include the cost, which is prohibitive for those below a certain income, the inconvenience of Internet cafés, and the general slowness and unreliability of Internet connections anywhere in the country. Some Internet cafés ask for patrons' ID cards or passports so they can register their names and make a note of which computers they used, for passing on to government officials who might come around requesting these lists; whether or not they let you use the computers if you refuse to comply depends entirely on the leniency of the employee.

There is a wireless network covering parts of Syria that can be accessed with the purchase of a special wireless modem from MTN or Syriatel, the cell phone service providers, but these modems cost the equivalent of over US $100 and subscribers pay for their traffic on an expensive per-gigabyte basis. It's very difficult to get high-speed Internet installed at home, but easy to use the slow dial-up service through your landline.

CONCLUSION

Syria has lain at a pivotal juncture throughout its long history; not for nothing did so many invading forces seek control of the country, only to be forced out a generation later by the next rising power. Today, Syria is just as critically placed, but it is perhaps a more independent state than before, having carefully constructed the web of alliances that make it possible to maintain a sovereign foreign policy in a region that great powers love to dominate. Syria is now a major regional player whose political hand seems only to be growing stronger.

This is also a dynamic country. It is in the midst not only of a significant economic transition, but also of a slower social transition, with rising numbers of women obtaining higher education and more young people generating their own ideas about what they want, then taking part in achieving it. It is a common visitor's fallacy to assume that what one sees is what there always was, so remember that the Syria that you will encounter on your visit is not exactly the same as the one you would have observed five, ten, or fifteen years ago.

Internally, it can be easy to look at Syria and see only what there is not: an open political system, an efficient economy. But in fact, Syria has a wealth of potential. The education system may not produce much original research, but it has not only gone far toward eradicating illiteracy—it provides a free college education for many, and produces competent professionals in several fields. The health system may not promise the most advanced techniques, but it provides decent primary care for all citizens. Reform may seem to occur with all the speed and energy of a tortoise, but that doesn't mean that it *doesn't* occur, or that there aren't people working for it on many fronts.

Such institutional and political factors make Syria strong, but it's the patience, humor, openness, pride, and community spirit of the Syrians themselves that make the country worth knowing.

Fascinating countries, like skilled actors, are the ones that seem to have it all—both beauty and depth. Syria is alluring, but interesting enough not be trivialized by being reduced to its looks. It's big enough to contain what seem to be contradictions—tradition and modernity, past and present, division and unity—and yet meld them into a whole. When you look closer, they may not be contradictions at all: they are precisely what make Syria itself.

Further Reading

Ball, Warwick. *Syria: A Historical and Architectural Guide.* Northampton, Mass.: Interlink Books, 1994.

Batatu, Hanna. *Syria's Peasantry, the Descendants of its Lesser Rural Notables, and Their Politics.* Princeton, New Jersey: Princeton University Press, 1999.

Burns, Ross. *Damascus: A History.* New York: Routledge, 2005.

Dalrymple, William. *From the Holy Mountain: A Journey among the Christians of the Middle East.* New York: Henry Holt and Company, 1997.

Dweck, Poopa. *Aromas of Aleppo: The Legendary Cuisine of Syrian Jews.* New York: Ecco, 2007.

George, Alan. *Syria: Neither Bread nor Freedom.* New York: Zed Books, 2003.

Qabbani, Nizar. *Arabian Love Poems.* Boulder, Colorado: Lynne Rienner Publishers, 1998.

Schami, Rafik. *The Dark Side of Love.* Northampton, Mass.: Interlink Publishing Group, 2009.

Seale, Patrick. *Asad of Syria: The Struggle for the Middle East.* Berkeley, Cal.: University of California Press, 1988.

Tamer, Zakaria. *Breaking Knees: Modern Arabic Short Stories from Syria.* Reading, UK: Garnett Publishing, 2008.

Van Dam, Nikolaos. *The Struggle for Power in Syria: Politics and Society under Asad and the Ba'ath Party.* New York: St. Martin's Press, 1979.

Index

culture smart! syria

Acknowledgments

I am grateful to the following individuals for their help, advice, thoughts, and insights: Hazem Katabi, Grace Chang, Ammar Hallaj, Sate Hamza, Rula Sayyaf, Anas Qtiesh, Ghada Hussein, Adam Coogle, Rachel Levine; and most of all, to my family and to my parents, Emily and Myles Standish, for all their love and support.